OSTFRONT

HITLER'S WAR ON RUSSIA 1941–45

CHARLES WINCHESTER

OSTFRONT

HITLER'S WAR ON RUSSIA 1941–45

First published in Great Britain in 2000
by Osprey Publishing, Elms Court, Chapel Way,
Botley, Oxford, OX2 9LP, UK
Email: osprey@osprey-publishing.co.uk

ISBN 1 84176 066 8

Military Editors: Lee Johnson and Nikolai Bogdanovic
Design: The Black Spot

Origination by Valhaven Ltd, Isleworth, UK
Printed through World Print Ltd, Hong Kong

00 01 02 03 04   10 9 8 7 6 5 4 3 2 1

FOR A CATALOGUE OF ALL BOOKS PUBLISHED BY
OSPREY MILITARY, AUTOMOTIVE AND AVIATION,
PLEASE WRITE TO:

The Marketing Manager,
Osprey Direct, PO Box 140, Wellingborough,
Northants NN8 4ZA, UK
Email: info@OspreyDirect.co.uk

The Marketing Manager,
Osprey Direct USA, PO Box 130, Sterling Heights,
MI 48311-0130, USA
Email: info@OspreyDirectUSA.com

or visit Osprey's Homepage at
http://www.osprey-publishing.co.uk

AUTHOR'S NOTE

Although the Germans referred to their opponents as 'Russian', the Soviet army was drawn from all the constituent republics of the USSR. It seems perverse to label them all 'Russian' today, now that so many of them are independent nations. The USSR's ground forces were still officially known as the Red Army until 1944 when they were re-titled the Soviet army. On the other hand, even President Gorbachev could slip up in public and say 'Russian' when it was politically correct to say 'Soviet', and the following account errs the same way.

Place names present further difficulty. Since the Polish frontier was shifted westwards by Stalin after the war, many towns and cities now have different names. The Soviets seized the Königsberg area for themselves, and the Kaliningrad enclave is a geographic anomaly waiting to be resolved today. Many German names in the Baltic republics have changed too; and of course, Leningrad has reverted to St. Petersburg. Modern maps of the independent Ukraine have Ukrainian names, not the traditional Russian ones. The industrial city known to western readers as Kharkov is more correctly rendered Char'kov from Russian, and becomes Harkiv when transliterated from Ukrainian. So, with an inconsistency that only an editor can really appreciate, I have tried to use the names most familiar to western readers.

Statistics are at once unavoidable and unreliable. The War in the East was won as much on the factory floor as on the battlefield, but few studies of German and Soviet wartime production agree on manufacturing totals. And when they do concur, further investigation sometimes uncovers a bogus source accepted for so long it has become 'fact'. In the city of London it has been said that there are three sorts of economists: those that can count, and those that can't. In his prescient analysis of late 20th century politics, *All the Trouble in the World*, P.J. O'Rourke notes how the OECD accepts (with a straight face) figures for population growth in Bangladesh to a hundredth decimal point. It is 'the first law of the social sciences, "The more precise the figure, the more general the lie".'

If absolutely accurate production figures ever emerge, authors can stop going cross-eyed trying to read old microfiche. Until they do, the following figures are as fair a comparison as can be assembled. In any case, the salient point is that the USSR built more T-34s than all the Pz. IIs, Pz. IIIs, Pz. IVs, Panthers and Tigers put together. The USA built more M-4 Shermans than the combined total of German tank production too. With almost all European industry under its control, the German war economy failed miserably to provide the weapons its army needed.

CONTENTS

INTRODUCTION

For many German families, World War II is synonymous with the Russian front. It was where the overwhelming majority of German servicemen fought, and where most of their 3.9 million dead lie buried.[1] In 1945 the Russian front came to Germany, engulfing East Prussia, Saxony and surging west all the way to the Elbe, while two million Soviet soldiers stormed Berlin, would-be capital of Hitler's 'Thousand Year Reich'.

In Russia World War II is known as 'The Great Patriotic War'. If the war only became truly 'patriotic' after the invaders were exposed as genocidal enslavers, and not the liberators many people had hoped them to be, there was no doubting its great scale. Hitler's invasion pitted the largest national armies ever assembled against each other. The front stretched from the Arctic Circle to the shores of the Black Sea. Battles took place over unprecedented distances: the gap smashed in the German lines by the Soviet winter offensive in December 1942 was wider than the entire western front in World War I.

It is salutary to compare the scale of operations on the Russian front with those in western Europe. In August 1944 38 Allied divisions fighting on a 120km front in France encircled 20 German divisions and, after 27 days' fighting, took about 90,000 prisoners. At the same time the Soviet forces mounted three offensives. Along the borders of Romania, 92 Soviet divisions and 6 tank/mechanised corps attacked 47 German and Romanian divisions on a frontage of about 700km, encircling 18 German divisions and taking 100,000 prisoners in a week. Meanwhile, 86 Soviet divisions and 10 tank/mechanised corps were attacking into southern Poland, destroying nearly 40 German divisions in the process. The third Soviet offensive, which had been underway since 22 June, involved 172 divisions and 12 tank/mechanised corps in an advance of 600km along a 1,000km front: 67 German divisions were overwhelmed in the battle, 17 never to reappear on the German order of battle.

By late 1944 91 Allied divisions in France, Belgium and the Netherlands, faced 65 German

RIGHT *A column of German armour passes through a village near Kursk, March 1942. During its first winter in Russia, the German army had already come to depend on the horse-drawn* panje: *its own transport system had collapsed.(R. Tomasi)*

LEFT *Dead bodies no longer excite interest in Leningrad's Nevski Prospekt at the beginning of the siege that was to cost the lives of over 600,000 people. Supply lines cut by the Germans, the population endured two winters with little food, fuel or medical supplies. (Library of Congress)*

divisions across a 400km front. In the east, 560 Soviet divisions were fighting 235 German divisions across a 3,200km front, and driving them rapidly westwards. Thus there is a strong argument that the Soviet Union had already won the war by 1944, whether the western Allies finally opened a second front or not.[2]

The human cost of the war is difficult for Americans or western Europeans to imagine. To compare the scale of casualties, about 2.5 per cent of the British population was killed or injured during World War II; American casualties were 0.6 per cent. In the USSR the proportion was no less than 25 per cent. Another statistic gives pause for thought. Twice as many soldiers were killed on the eastern front in 1941–45 than in all the theatres of war of 1914–18 put together.

Neither side limited its killing to military personnel: the Soviet war-dead total of over 20 million includes at least seven million civilians. The War in the East was a medieval war of conquest conducted with twentieth-century technology. It was Hitler's war: there was no prospect of it ending in a conventional peace treaty. The German dictator intended far more than just moving a border here and annexing a province there. He was not going to accept reparation payments or negotiate a treaty, restricting the future size of the Red Army. Hitler planned nothing less than a war of extermination, eliminating the Communist regime, the Jews and indeed most of the peoples of Eastern Europe. The conquered territories would become German colonies, with new German cities linked to the Reich by autobahn and railroad, the Russian steppe dotted with German soldier-colonists establishing (like Roman legionaries of old) brave outposts of civilisation in a barbarous land.

The full extent of Hitler's grotesque war aims was only known to the upper echelons of the Nazi hierarchy. After the war, many German generals would persuade both the Nuremberg prosecutors and western military historians that they had not known. In 1945 British and American officers found it difficult to accept that fellow officers and gentlemen – who had fought a largely 'clean' war in the west – could have been implicated in the horrors being reported in the east. Unfortunately, more recent investigation has exposed the disagreeable truth that the German army was deeply implicated. Heinrich Himmler, chief executor of the 'Final Solution', described the Holocaust as 'a page of Glory in our history which has never been written and never is to be written'. However, the days are long past when the SS could serve as the alibi of a nation: German army and police units participated in the slaughter of Jews, gypsies, Communist government officials, their families and other civilians. So did the pro-German forces raised in the Baltic States, the Ukraine, Croatia, Slovakia, Romania and Hungary.

The Wehrmacht high command was invited to the Berghof by Hitler on the eve of the attack on Poland in 1939. The loss of so much German territory to Poland under the terms of the Versailles Treaty had never been accepted, and a war to recover these lands might well have been undertaken even if Hitler had never come to power. But Hitler invested the campaign with far more than territorial objectives. His address to the generals anticipated both the nature of German rule in the east and the nature of his war against the USSR:

RIGHT *From early 1942 the Red Army received tanks, aircraft and strategic resources from Britain and the USA, in this case a British Universal Carrier complete with Bren gun. (Author's collection)*

BELOW *Two veterans of the German 6th Army walk among the ruins of Stalingrad, which they were poised to capture in the autumn of 1942. The 6th Army included some of the toughest professional soldiers in the German forces: its fate that winter stunned the world and changed the course of the war. (Author's collection)*

'… in the East I have put my death's head formations in place with the command relentlessly and without compassion to send into death many women and children of Polish origin and language … Poland will be depopulated and settled with Germans … As for the rest … the fate of Russia will be exactly the same.'[3]

One officer recorded in his diary how Herman Göring literally danced with glee.

It is beyond doubt that the German army treated Soviet prisoners-of-war more cruelly than its Japanese allies dealt with Allied POWs in Burma and the Pacific. Of the approximately five million Soviet servicemen taken prisoner in World War II, over three million were killed. At his trial at Nuremberg, SS General von dem Bach-Zelewski said: 'If for decades, a doctrine is preached that the Slav race is an inferior race, and that the Jews are not even human at all, then such an explosion is inevitable'.

If the role of Adolf Hitler is central to the nature and the course of the War in the East, that of his enemy and eventual nemesis, Iosif Vissarionovich Dzhugashvili – or Stalin, as the world knew him – was hardly less important. There was considerable truth in the idea that 'only Stalin got us into this mess, and only Stalin can get us out', although it was not a sentiment to voice in public. Stalin bears unique responsibility for the weakness of the Soviet armed forces in 1941 and the readiness of the Russian/Ukrainian peasantry to welcome almost any foreign invader who promised to drive out the Communists and abolish the collective farms. It was on his orders that countless soldiers were sacrificed in premature, over-ambitious offensives beyond the operational abilities of the army that Stalin had beheaded in 1937. Yet as the war progressed, Stalin learned to listen to his best generals, to rely on them rather than the party apparatchiks whose political reliability was no substitute for military competence. Only Stalin could have forced through the industrialisation of the USSR in the 1930s with such brutal lack of concern over the human cost; but perhaps only Stalin could have orchestrated the removal to safety of so much

Soviet heavy industry after the German invasion. Enigmatic and inhuman, the workaholic Stalin never visited the front or a factory, indeed he seldom left the Kremlin. From his Spartan office there, he exerted a steadily more decisive grip on the war.

'Truth' the old proverb says 'is the daughter of Time', and only with the passage of years has a balanced account of Hitler's War in the East become feasible. Post-war Soviet accounts were created to feed the vanity of Stalin. As soon as the tide of battle had turned the ageing tyrant (who had never served in any army) proclaimed himself Commander-in-Chief. Successive 'histories' sought to demonstrate Stalin's military genius. After his death, Khruschev demanded similar treatment, necessitating complete revision of Soviet history; another radical overhaul followed his overthrow. After the 'decades of stagnation', President Mikhail Gorbachev swept away the surviving gerontocracy and instituted reforms that led to the disintegration of the Soviet empire that Stalin established in Eastern Europe. The Soviet Union outlasted that empire by less than two years, splintering along ancient national boundaries. In the process, the history of the Great Patriotic War has been liberated from the dead hand of Communist functionaries.

For the 50 years that the Soviet history of World War II was massaged to suit the ruling clique, western readers relied heavily on German accounts of the War in the East. Some are classics of war literature, others extremely valuable for the light they cast on German grand strategy. Yet, as will be seen, even a commander of indisputable brilliance like Von Manstein was capable of twisting the facts. His literary sleight of hand in

Lost Victories was as hard to detect as his shift of Panzer divisions to the south of Kharkov in 1943, and no less effective. The common impression given by German accounts is that the Soviets enjoyed enormous numerical and material superiority and that if it had not been for Hitler's lunatic decisions, the Russians could have been defeated. There is a degree of truth here, but it is far from the whole story. Some of the generals who advanced this thesis had also entertained the hope, fostered by Goebbels, that the western Allies might strike a deal with Hitler and join forces with the Wehrmacht against the 'Bolshevik hordes'.

An account of this size cannot cover every battle of the war in detail. I have not even attempted a uniform coverage. Certain battles, notably Stalingrad and Kursk, receive more extended treatment, while other major actions are relegated to a paragraph or two. Stalingrad and Kursk were recognised at the time as battles of special significance. The former was a defeat of unparalleled magnitude for the German army. Germany had accelerated its call-up to provide the manpower for its 1942 offensive in Russia: its complete and utter failure left the Ostheer no prospect of realising Hitler's boundless objectives in the east. Kursk was another disaster for the Germans: although the military losses there are often exaggerated, its political impact is beyond dispute. As successive Russian offensives drove back the front line in the late summer of 1943, Germany's allies opened negotiations with Moscow. Only inside the concrete bunkers of the 'Wolf's Lair' could you fail to know which way the wind was blowing.

CHAPTER ONE

HITLER AND THE WEHRMACHT 1941

'There's only one duty: to Germanise this country by the immigration of Germans and look upon the natives as Redskins'

Adolf Hitler

BELOW German preparations for the invasion of Russia were disrupted by Mussolini's attack on Greece, which came to an embarassing halt, forcing German intervention in April 1941. Here an SS reconnaissance unit negotiates a twisty mountain road. (Bundesarchiv)

After the war many German generals recorded their dismay and bewilderment that Germany had plunged into Russia in 1941 without defeating or making peace with Britain. For a generation of soldiers who had been junior officers in World War I, this was the height of foolishness. It was widely believed that Germany's defeat in 1918 was the result of fighting on two fronts at once. However, it is difficult to find much evidence that the generals opposed a two-front war in 1941. In fact the German army's senior leadership agreed that it would take a five month campaign to destroy the Soviet army, occupy the major cities of the western USSR and march into Moscow. Nor were they alone in this assessment: in London, the joint intelligence committee predicted that Moscow would fall within six months. In Washington, President Roosevelt received even earlier estimates of German victory.

POLITICAL BACKGROUND

Hitler's invasion of the Soviet Union was not an opportunist swipe at the last major opponent left on the board, prompted by his forces' inability to cross the English Channel. Since World War I he had dreamed of destroying Russia, seizing the western republics of the USSR as 'living space' (*lebensraum*) for a new German empire. It was sketched out interminably in *Mein Kampf*. German generals who expressed surprise that Hitler should order them to the east were being disingenuous. Perhaps they were maintaining the army's avowedly apolitical stance, adopted in the 1920s to mask its blind indifference to the fate of the Weimar democracy. In *Mein Kampf* Hitler stated several pre-conditions necessary for Germany to begin its drive to the east. He wanted an agreement with the British, alliance with the Italians and the destruction of France's military power. If the Führer added new justifications in 1940, claiming that the USSR represented an immediate military threat to Germany, he was really excusing himself from attempting the invasion of Britain. The only surprise in Hitler's policy towards the USSR had been his temporary alliance with Stalin, the Nazi-Soviet pact, that consigned Poland to oblivion in 1939. The idea of breaking this cynical pact grew in the late summer of 1940 as the Luftwaffe failed to subdue the RAF over southern England. Hitler's navy chief, Admiral Raeder expressed his deep unease at the proposed amphibious assault across the English Channel. Hitler prevaricated, conscious of the enormity of his decision.

While Hitler pondered his options, Mussolini ordered an invasion of his own. On 28 October 1940, the Italian army in Albania invaded Greece, Il Duce anticipating a grand Roman victory parade through Athens. It was not to be. The Greeks counter-attacked and drove their attackers back across the border.

In November Hitler was still unable to bring himself to issue the detailed orders requested by his generals. The OKH had been told to prepare for a Russian campaign, but no objectives or timetable had been laid down. This reflected Hitler's failure to persuade two potential allies to

join his crusade against Bolshevism. Hitler had tried to secure active military co-operation from Vichy France, but this had come to nothing. General Franco – whose forces had received so much aid from Germany and Italy in the civil war – stubbornly refused to allow Axis forces through Spain to attack Gibraltar. The most he would offer was a division of volunteers for service in Russia.

In December the Italian Army of Libya was demolished by a far smaller British and Commonwealth force. Italian soldiers surrendered in droves and Italy's African empire seemed poised to vanish. The Greeks continued to drive back the Italians in Albania. The future of the Fascist regime in Italy looked bleak.

Hitler realised that he would have to intervene to rescue his ally from the consequences of his folly. On 13 December he issued orders for the invasion of Greece, to take place early in the spring.

Five days later he issued Directive 21, ordering 'Operation Barbarossa', the invasion of Russia, to be launched on 15 May 1941. The objective was to destroy the Red Army in western Russia, armoured forces advancing rapidly to block any attempt to retreat into the hinterland. German forces were to push as far east as a line from Archangel to the River Volga, bringing the remaining Russian industries in the Urals within range of the Luftwaffe.

The German diversion to Greece turned into an offensive throughout the Balkans after a *coup*

d'état in Belgrade. Prince Paul, the regent of Yugoslavia had made his peace with Hitler, signing a pact with Germany and allowing German troops passage for their forthcoming assault. But the Yugoslav army, led by General Simovic seized power on the night of 26-7 March in the name of the young King Peter. Simovic actually intended to steer a more neutral path, rather than throw in his lot with the British and Greeks, but Hitler did not wait to speak to him. The German forces were ordered to attack with 'merciless harshness'.

The invasion of Greece and Yugoslavia began on 6 April, the systematic terror bombing of Belgrade killing 17,000 people. Yugoslavia surrendered on 17 April, Greece surrendered on 20 April, and the British Commonwealth forces that had landed in Greece began yet another withdrawal to the sea, hammered by German air attacks. At the same time, a detachment of German mechanised troops deployed to Italy's aid in North Africa launched its counter-attack. Under the inspiring leadership of Erwin Rommel, the Germans drove the British back into Egypt.

The Balkan adventure had been another spectacular triumph for German arms, but it imposed a significant delay on the invasion of Russia. At the end of May Operation Barbarossa was postponed until 22 June.

HITLER AND BLITZKRIEG 1939–40

The staggering success of Blitzkrieg in Poland in September 1939 and then France and the Low Countries in 1940 took everyone by surprise. No army in Europe had managed to resist the combination of Panzer divisions and dive bombers – the

LEFT *From left to right: private, Hungarian infantry, 1942; major, Hungarian cavalry, 1941; major-general, 1942. Hungary declared war on the USSR a week after the German invasion and supplied few troops in 1941, Romania still being regarded as the main enemy. In 1942 Hungary sent its 2nd Army to join Army Group South and it was heavily defeated during the Stalingrad campaign. (Mike Chappell, from Men-at-Arms 131, Germany's Eastern Front Allies 1941–45)*

BELOW *A PzKpfw IV Ausf.D of 6.Pz.-Div., in action in Russia, 1941. Pre-war plans called for Panzer IVs to form a quarter of the tank strength of each Panzer division, but there were not enough available in 1941. The 6th Panzer Division was assigned to Army Group North in the initial invasion. (David Smith)*

RIGHT *Germany invaded Yugoslavia after the Yugoslav army organised a coup, ousting Prince Paul who had signed a pact with Hitler. The country was overrun and a bitter guerrilla war began, old scores from which were to be settled in the 1990s.(R. Tomasi)*

BELOW *A PzKpfw 35(t) of II/Pz.-Regt. 11, 6.Pz.-Div, in action in Russia during 1941. The only serious drawback with the PzKpfw 35(t) was its rivetted construction that would shower the crew with splinters if the turret was struck by a heavy projectile. (Terry Hadler, from* New Vanguard 26, German Light Panzers *1932–42)*

position as Von Rundstedt's chief of staff for advocating this strategy, and was posted to an infantry corps in the rear. Hitler's generals had recommended a scaled-down Schlieffen plan, with the main offensive blow delivered through Belgium – just as the Allied commanders assumed they would. Hitler overruled them, gambling that Guderian's radical scheme for an offensive through the Ardennes would work.

The great victory in France had two important consequences, neither of which would be apparent until German forces were deep inside the Soviet Union in 1941. Firstly, the German high command believed that their Blitzkrieg tactics represented nothing less than a military revolution: a clear break with the experience of World War I when the defence had held every advantage. Blitzkrieg reversed the situation. Fast-moving tank formations with air support could bypass centres of resistance, drive deep behind the front line and overwhelm the defence. The parallel with the stormtroop tactics of 1918 was not accidental. Unfortunately for Germany, the similarities between the *Kaiserschlacht* and Operation Barbarossa would not end there. Hitler shared the generals' conviction that the technology and tactical methods that brought victory in France had universal application. Yet he drew a second conclusion; that his intuitive leadership, grounded in his front-line experiences in World War I, gave him a unique insight into military affairs. It was he who had insisted on the victorious strategy of 1940, not the general staff. When the campaign in Russia began to falter in 1941, Hitler would have the confidence to overrule his commanders again, eventually appointing himself as the Commander-in-Chief.

THE GERMAN ARMED FORCES IN 1941

The overwhelming bulk of the German army consisted of foot soldiers. In June 1941 the German army fielded 175 infantry divisions, 21 Panzer divisions and 15 motorised infantry divisions. Two-thirds of the infantry divisions that took part in the invasion of Russia relied on horse-drawn wagons to carry their supplies. Most field artillery batteries were horse-drawn too, so the infantry marched at the same pace as their fathers did in 1914. They were not able to use the railways, as it took months to convert the Russian wide-gauge track, and the Soviets evacuated or destroyed most of their rolling stock. So in fact the strategic mobility of most German units was no greater than that of Napoleon Bonaparte's '*Grande Armée*' of 1812.

German infantry divisions consisted of three

Germans had apparently perfected the recipe for victory. What the defeated Allies did not know is that the speed and apparent ease of the German success was as much of a surprise to most German officers as to their enemies. The breakthrough in 1940, the armoured offensive through the Ardennes and subsequent storming of the Meuse had been opposed by the general staff. General von Manstein had been demoted from his

LEFT *The Yugoslav air force was wiped out in days, leaving the Luftwaffe free to bomb Belgrade in a deliberate act of terror demanded by Hitler. (R. Tomasi)*

BELOW *A concrete strongpoint on the Siegfried line that defended Germany's border with France. Gambling that Britain and France would not attack in 1939, Hitler left only token forces in the west while his army crushed Poland. (R. Tomasi)*

infantry regiments, each of three battalions, and an artillery regiment with 36 105mm guns and 12 150mm guns. The anti-tank *abteillung* consisted of three companies, each of 12 37mm guns. The infantry battalions had three infantry companies (about 180 men), a machine gun company – three pairs of 7.92mm general purpose machine guns – and a mortar company with three pairs of 81mm mortars.

The Panzer divisions had been reorganised since the French campaign, their tank strength reduced to free enough vehicles to double the number of divisions. By June 1941, each Panzer division included two or three battalions of tanks (with an average total strength of about 150 vehicles); four (sometimes six) battalions of truck–mounted infantry (designated Panzergrenadier in 1942); one reconnaissance battalion on motorcycles; an artillery regiment with 36 105mm guns; three self-propelled anti-tank companies with a dozen or so 37mm or 50mm guns mounted on obsolete tank chassis; plus armoured reconnaissance squadrons, engineer and anti-aircraft companies.

German tank regiments were supposed to include two companies of PzKpfw IIIs, armed with 37mm or 50mm guns, and one company of PzKpfw IVs with a short barrelled 75mm gun intended for direct fire support of the infantry. However, in 1941 the Panzer divisions fielded a total of 3,648 tanks (as opposed to the 2,445 of

1940) but only 1,000 were PzKpfw IIIs and there were only about 450 PzKpfw IVs. Although the diminutive PzKpfw I had disappeared from front-line service, many tank battalions were still equipped with PzKpfw IIs (armed with a 20mm gun) and others relied on the Czech-built PzKpfw 35 and PzKpfw 38(t).

The motorised infantry divisions were smaller than the standard divisions; six infantry battalions in trucks, with artillery towed by lorries or tracked

ABOVE *A German machine gun team equipped with the MG08 seen during late 1939: but for minor details of uniform, this could be a scene from the 1914–18 war. Although Hitler had devoted the German economy to war production since the mid-1930s, modernisation was far from complete when war broke out. (US National Archives)*

RIGHT *German stormtroops seen during the second battle of the Marne, July 1918, which led to Germany's defeat in the First World War. German tactics in 1940 drew heavily on the methods of 1918; the use of élite units to spearhead the attack, infiltration tactics and close air support. (Imperial War Museum – hereafter referred to as the IWM)*

prime movers. Their reconnaissance units included motorcycles and armoured cars. In 1942 a battalion of self-propelled guns or tanks was added, and half-track armoured personnel carriers appeared in greater numbers, but in the initial campaign they were essentially infantry units, albeit with greater mobility.

The Luftwaffe had made an enormous contribution to the German victory in France. During the critical breakthrough at Sedan, the German armoured commanders had gambled that air power could substitute for the heavy artillery they

would not have time to push through the Ardennes forest. While Messerschmitt Bf109s dominated the Allied fighters, German twin-engine bombers and Junkers Ju-87 Stukas delivered accurate bombing attacks that knocked out most French artillery and pulverised strong points defending the Meuse. The massive French heavy tanks, armoured leviathans immune to infantry anti-tank guns, were destroyed by air attacks while on trains carrying them to the front.

The close co-ordination between ground and air forces was to be repeated in the attack on Russia. Yet German production policy was so haphazard that the losses over France and in the Battle of Britain had not been made good. Hitler launched the attack on the USSR with about 200 fewer aircraft than he had been able to deploy for the attack in the west in 1940. The Luftwaffe had a total of 1,945 aircraft available for Operation Barbarossa (Luftflotte 3 had some 660 aircraft in France and Belgium, 190 aircraft were retained for defence of German airspace, Luftflotte 5 was in Norway and the 10th Air Corps in the Mediterranean). The total included 150 transports and about 80 liaison aircraft. About 1,400 combat aircraft took part in the initial attack on 22 June: 510 twin-engine bombers (Dornier Do-17, Junkers Ju-88, Heinkel He-111); 290 Junkers Ju-87 dive-bombers; 440 Messerschmitt Bf109 single engine fighters; 40 Messerschmitt Bf110 twin-engine fighters; 120 reconnaissance aircraft (Junkers Ju-86, Focke-Wulf Fw 189, etc.)

German allies provided nearly 1,000 additional machines, but of varying quality. Finland

17

Two aspects of the German air force deserve comment here. There were no four-engined heavy bombers of the sort entering service in the USA and UK; promising designs like the Dornier Do-19 and Junkers Ju-19 had been cancelled in 1937. The Heinkel He-177, the only heavy bomber under development, was hamstrung by a demand for dive bombing capability and would never be successful. Long range attacks on Soviet industrial centres – or the rail network – would not be possible. Secondly, the provision of fewer than 200 transport aircraft to service military forces from the Baltic sea to the Crimea was clearly inadequate.

GROUND FORCES FOR OPERATION BARBAROSSA

Almost a third of German infantry divisions remained in western and southern Europe, leaving 120 for the invasion of Russia. They were supported by 14 Finnish, 14 Romanian, four Italian, and two Slovak divisions. Spain provided enough volunteers to create the Azul (Blue) division, which was incorporated into the German army as the 250th Division in July 1941. Hungary provided its 'Rapid Corps' of three brigades, including 160 light tanks. The allied contingents were a useful source of extra manpower but multiplied Germany's existing logistic problems. They all had different equipment, requiring different sets of spares, and German units were already filled

had 230 fighters, 41 bombers and 36 dedicated ground-attack aircraft; Romania provided 423 aircraft and Italy supplied about 100 aircraft to support its forces attached to Army Group South in July 1941. The Hungarian contingent was backed by two air regiments; together with the Croatian Air Legion, this added another 60 aircraft.

LEFT Crew members of the German Panzerwaffe, in action in Russia, 1941–2. From left to right: oberwachtmeister, Pz.-Regt.24; obergefreiter, Panzertruppe; gefreiter, Aufklärungstruppe. Two carry the gasoline cans soon to be christened 'jerrycans' by the British in the western desert. The Panzer divisions carried nearly double their normal fuel supply for the invasion of Russia, but it was still not enough. (Richard Hook, from Men-at-Arms 24, The Panzer Divisions)

BELOW A moving carpet of flies swarms across the dead in a German position on the western front, 1917. This was a familiar sight to Adolf Hitler who won the Iron Cross 1st class while serving with 16th Bavarian Reserve Infantry Regiment. Hitler exhibited great personal bravery on the battlefield, but he was recognised as odd and not promoted beyond corporal. Hitler's front line experiences led him to insist on rigid defensive methods that would be the downfall of his army in Russia. (Author's collection)

RIGHT *In April 1940 Hitler took another military gamble, ordering the invasion of Norway despite the overwhelming naval superiority of the Allies. It paid off. Here German soldiers prepare to disembark, with the cruiser* Admiral Hipper *in the background. (US National Archives)*

FAR RIGHT *A PzBefw 38(t) Ausf.B command tank of 8.Pz.-Div, in action in Russia 1941. (Terry Hadler, from New Vanguard 26,* German Light Panzers 1932–42)

BELOW *Air power was the key to German success in Norway and France in 1940: bombers like this Heinkel He-111 were able to operate with virtual impunity as the superb German fighter arm won air superiority in a matter of days. (R. Tomasi)*

out with a staggering variety of captured vehicles. Motor transport units drove a mixture of lorries drawn from all over German-occupied Europe. Most of the allied forces did not cross the Soviet frontier until July, and many were used for rear area security when they did. German strategy also had to ensure that the mutually hostile Hungarian and Romanian contingents were kept apart. (They had spent much of the 1930s preparing to fight each other.)

LEFT *A Panzer II halted by a demolished bridge in France, June 1940. Note the aerial recognition panel on the rear deck. Allied tanks and artillery units were defeated by air attack before they even reached the battlefields. (IWM)*

CENTRE *A Czech-built Panzer 38(t) seen in action in 1940. By 1941 the German tank force was about a third larger than that used against France, thanks largely to the extra 941 tanks obtained from Czech factories. But the theatre of war was vastly greater. (Author's collection)*

BOTTOM *German troops crossing a river with their 3.7cm anti-tank guns during the invasion of Belgium. Hitler overruled his senior officers in 1940, risking a bold strategy promoted by Von Manstein and Guderian. The original German strategy had been a cautious push into the Low Countries. (Library of Congress)*

The postponement of Barbarossa caused by the Balkan campaign was once advanced as an explanation for the ensuing failure of the campaign in 1941. In fact the spring thaw came late that year, reducing most roads to a sea of liquid mud throughout May, so an earlier assault was unlikely to have made much faster progress. However, the Balkan campaign involved a lot of mileage for German motor transport and tanks. Kleist's 1st Panzer Group, the cutting edge of Army Group South, would begin Barbarossa with nearly a third of its tanks at workshops in Germany. The airborne invasion of Crete had been a pyrrhic victory for the Luftwaffe, with the effective destruction of its élite 7th Airborne Division. The airborne assault on Crete had been extremely costly in aircraft as well as paratroopers: 146 Junkers Ju-52s were destroyed and another 150 damaged in May 1941. This spelt the end – at least in the short term – of German airborne operations. The possible contribution of Germany's superbly-trained paratroopers to Barbarossa is one of the more intriguing 'what if's of the campaign. One mission discussed before the battle for Crete was for airborne forces to help the Panzer divisions hold the outer ring of a 'pocket' until the infantry could arrive; something that the hard-pressed mechanised forces might have found valuable in the summer of 1941.[4] In the event, the reconstituted airborne division was employed as conventional infantry on the Leningrad front from late 1941 to early 1943.

German hopes rested on a relatively small section of the total forces deployed. The success or

ABOVE *Two contrasting views of Hitler's army entering Bulgaria in March 1941. The highly-engineered SdKfz 251 half-track epitomises the modern image German propaganda played on, but the horse-drawn transport column is more typical. Most of the German army was no more mobile than that of 1914. (US National Archives and R. Tomasi)*

RIGHT *Of the 2,500 tanks used by the Germans in 1940, 955 were Panzer IIs armed with a 20mm gun. There were still over 1,000 in service when the Germans invaded Russia in 1941, some 750 taking part in the initial campaign. (US National Archives)*

ABOVE *British army
transport and civilian
vehicles shunted aside
on a French highway
in 1940. German
mechanised forces had
been able to exploit an
excellent network of
metalled roads in France,
but communications were
far more primitive in
Russia. (R. Tomasi)*

failure of Hitler's planned knock-out blow in Russia would depend on 19 Panzer divisions. (Two, the 15th and 21st, were with Rommel in North Africa.) Their task would be to repeat their success of 1940, breaking through the enemy front line to trap his forces between the hammer and anvil. Thanks to the reorganisation there were now twice as many Panzer divisions as in 1940, but they would be operating over a vastly greater area. Paris is little more than 200 miles from the German frontier. On 21 May 1940 the front line extended from the Channel coast to the Meuse – a distance of about 250 miles. Yet in Russia the front line would expand from 800 miles to about 1,500 as the Germans reached Moscow. The supply lines would stretch back for 1,000 miles.

The German forces had many strengths: combat experience in Poland and France allied to excellent training methods had created a highly professional army, brimming with confidence. The Luftwaffe had one of the world's best fighter aircraft, and its aircrew were superbly-trained. Morale was extremely high, and from the front-line soldiers to the General Staff there were few men who doubted Hitler's judgement when he said that one good kick would bring down the whole rotten edifice of Russian Communism. The weaknesses of the German forces were less

evident: there were no new bomber aircraft being developed to replace the existing fleet, the tanks were neither well armed nor well protected by comparison with the latest Soviet types, mechanised units were equipped with dozens of different types of vehicles which shared few common parts and had to be returned to Germany for maintenance. Above all, Hitler effectively had two armies; a small mechanised force of some 35 divisions and a large unmechanised mass dependent on horse transport.

Nevertheless, the Germans planned to win victory in the east in one intensive Blitzkrieg campaign. Since the Russians would be beaten before their famously cold winter set in – enough senior officers had served on the eastern front in World War I to remember just how cold it could be – OKH decreed that the army would not require winter clothing. Some cold weather gear was ordered, but only for the 60 or so divisions earmarked for occupation duties. Only one top commander demurred - Field Marshal Milch quietly ignored a direct order from Hitler and set about organising winter uniforms for all 800,000 Luftwaffe personnel he suspected would still be needed in Russia as the snows started to fall.

CHAPTER TWO

THE RED ARMY

How can you have a revolution without firing squads?

V.I. Lenin

RIGHT *Two examples of Soviet planes. Above: MiG-3 of 7.IAP, summer 1941. Below: I-16 Tip 18 (mod), September 1941. The MiG-3 was a new type, only entering service in late 1940, but its armament of one 12.7mm and two 7.62mm machine guns was too weak, and its performance also disappointing. Only about 3,000 were built. The I-16 had been in service since 1934 but although manoeuvrable to the point of being unstable, it was too slow to survive against Bf-109s. Production ceased in 1942 after over 8,000 had been built. (John Weal, from* Aircraft of the Aces 15, Soviet Aces of World War II)

BELOW *Soviet and German troops shake hands over the body of Poland, 1939. The unholy alliance came as a surprise to the German and Soviet peoples and armies alike, although in the 1920s there had been close co-operation between the Red Army and the Reichswehr. (Author's collection)*

To meet the German invasion, the Soviet Union had 171 infantry divisions in the western USSR, with new armies assembling further east along the Dnepr and Dvina rivers. There were 20 mechanised corps, very 'tank heavy' formations, each with two tank divisions (with a total authorised strength of 750–1,000 tanks), a truck-borne infantry regiment and supporting troops. However, the corps organisation had only just been introduced, many corps had their component divisions widely separated, and few had ever functioned together. Few if any of the tank divisions were at full strength. Their vehicles were mostly light tanks, poorly protected and thinly armoured: lacking radios they communicated with signal flags, and low standards of maintenance would see many of them breaking down the moment they had to deploy in June 1941.

The standard Soviet infantry division was similar to the German: nine battalions in three regiments, with an artillery regiment of 36 guns (theoretically 24 76mm guns and 12 122mm howitzers) and supporting troops. However, most divisions were significantly under strength in the summer of 1941, averaging only 8,000 men

SOVIET AIR POWER 1941[5]

European Russia	Modern type	Obsolete	Total
reconnaissance aircraft		620	
fighters	2,000 (I-16)	980	
bombers	1,100 (SB-2)		
	1,000 (DB-3)		
transport/liaison aircraft		1,800	
subtotal	4,100 +	3,400	= 7,500
Far East	1,000	2,000	= 3,000
	5,100 +	5,400	= 10,500

against an authorised strength of 14,483.

Unlike the Luftwaffe, the Soviet air force was not an independent force. The Red Army had over 10,000 aircraft, but many were obsolete and serviceability was poor (about 50 per cent).

Since few had radios and there was no radar system to co-ordinate them, tactics were primitive. Barrier patrols of the sort flown in World War I absorbed large numbers of aircraft but were not effective, and the pilots were trained to fly the sort of tight formations that the RAF had favoured in 1939 – a system rapidly discredited in action against the loose formations of German fighters.

In terms of total mobilised strength, the Soviet and German forces were on a par, with about three million men each, although the Soviet Union had another million personnel between Moscow, the Caucasus, Siberia and the frontier with Japanese-occupied Manchuria. Yet in Germany, it was assumed the numbers would not matter. General Halder's intelligence summary to Hitler concluded that the Red Army was leaderless.

During the last three years, Stalin had ordered the execution of almost all his senior military officers, and an astonishing proportion of junior commanders too; three out of five Marshals of the Soviet Union, all eleven deputy defence commissars, the commander of every military district, 14 out of 16 army commanders, 60 out of 67 corps commanders, 136 out of 199 division commanders and half of all regimental commanders. In numerical terms 40,000 officers from a total strength of about 80,000 were arrested, and 15,000 were shot. While the pace of the slaughter had slowed after 1939, the terror had yet to run its full course. The disastrous campaign against Finland in the winter of 1939–40 led to new arrests for treason at a number of bases. Failure at the front was dealt with in summary Bolshevik

ABOVE LEFT A Soviet T-26 tank supplied to the Republican forces during the Spanish Civil War. General Pavlov's experiences there led to the break-up of the Red Army's massed tank formations in the late 1930s. Nearly half of the Soviet tank brigades had T-26s in 1940. (IWM)

ABOVE The Polikarpov I-16 was a revolutionary design in its day, the first monoplane with retractable undercarriage to enter service as a fighter. It performed well in the Spanish Civil War, but although highly manoeuverable and well armed, it was too slow to survive against the Messerschmitt Bf-109s in 1941. (R. Tomasi)

LEFT T-37 amphibious light tanks seen during an exercise in the 1930s. Stalin saw to it that the Red Army had more tanks than all other armies put together, but by 1941 most were obsolete and maintenance problems left more than half of them unfit for service. (IWM)

style, 'the discipline of the revolver'. The commander of the 44th Infantry Division extricated a few survivors from a Finnish encirclement, only to be shot on the orders of Stalin's henchman Lev Mekhlis.

Nearly 200 years previously, Voltaire observed that the occasional execution of an admiral is necessary to encourage the others, but the wholesale massacre of the Soviet officer corps drastically reduced the effectiveness of its armed forces. At the time of the German invasion only a quarter of Red Army officers had been in their jobs for more than 12 months. The purge was so comprehensive that most senior positions were filled by men out of their professional depth. Only 7.6 per cent of the surviving officers had a higher military education, most had a secondary education and nothing more.[6] The purge exterminated a generation of officers who had developed armoured forces, integrated with air power and even paratroops and had gained combat experience since the Russian Civil War. As Khruschev observed after Stalin's death, 'the cadre of leaders who gained military experience in Spain and the Far East was almost completely liquidated … the policy led also to undermined military discipline, because for several years officers of all ranks and even soldiers in the Party and Komsomol cells were taught to 'unmask' their superiors as hidden enemies.'[7] Fear

verging on paranoia left most officers afraid to do anything other than literally obey written orders. Anyone exercising 'initiative' was likely to feel the cold muzzle of a pistol on the back of their neck.

STALIN'S USSR

The Soviet Union was a very different Russia from the country Germany had defeated in 1917. On the eastern front in World War I, Russian armies were much less well equipped than their German opponents. Poor procurement decisions – huge fortresses packed with siege artillery, but not enough field guns – rather than lack of heavy industry[8] handicapped them from the start. In their early battles in 1941 the Germans found the Red Army similarly inferior, but the tables were turning even as the Panzer divisions fought their way to the outskirts of Moscow.

Russian industry had been transformed under the communist regime: coal and steel production vastly exceeded pre-1914 levels and gigantic new factories like the tank plant at Kharkov were not just building more tanks than Germany, they were building better ones. Soviet tank production in the early 1930s exceeded 3,000 tanks a year. German production was only 2,200 per annum as late as 1940. The later BT tanks and the T-26 carried 37mm and later 45mm guns, and the T-34 and KV-1 entering production in 1940 were superior

to any German tank either in service or on the drawing board. Stalin's crash industrialisation programme began with the 1928 Five Year Plan. Yet these giant strides in heavy industry had been achieved at terrible human cost. Working conditions were as bad as anything Marx had encountered in nineteenth-century industrial slums, although Stalin's dark mills were on a truly satanic scale. Unrealistic production quotas were set, and then increased. Failure was not an option, so the systematic faking of production statistics began – and became a permanent feature of Soviet-style industry. A more rational, humane strategy might have brought greater results, but the cold-blooded ideologue in the Kremlin knew no other method than terror. The political, military and psychological consequences of Stalinism would profoundly affect the War in the East.

Like a number of his fellow Bolshevik revolutionaries, Iosif Vissarionovich Dzhugashvili adopted a pseudonym. His choice of 'Stalin' – 'Man of Steel' – says a great deal about his self-image. Jailed several times by the Tsarist authorities, Stalin was a professional revolutionary who never actually held down a job in his life. After Lenin's death in 1923, many senior figures in the Communist Party imagined themselves to be part of a collective leadership, but Stalin manoeuvred them all aside. By the time of the German invasion, Stalin had been the undisputed dictator of the Soviet Union for nearly 20 years. Indeed, such was the machiavellian subtlety of his rise to power that it is difficult to identify when his 'rule' actually began.

While Soviet industrial output soared, agricultural productivity slumped. Since the overwhelming bulk of the Soviet population lived in small villages, and most of the Red Army was recruited from the countryside – as well as most senior commanders who survived the purges,[9] the young men that faced the German invader were still living with the consequences of 'collectivisation'. Peasant farms were reorganised into Collective Farms with merciless enthusiasm by Party officials. Kulaks (the marginally better-off peasants) were to be 'liquidated' as 'class enemies'. The reign of terror across the Russian countryside touched every village, and although grain was still shipped into the cities, there was widespread starvation, particularly in the Ukraine. Several million people died in the years of famine, millions of others were alive in 1941 only because they had survived by eating grass, shoe leather or even human flesh.

Most of the Bolshevik leadership came from urban backgrounds and had an almost superstitious fear of Russia's peasant population. The peasant soldiers of 1914 had practically worshipped the Tsar and the Communist regime meant little to rural communities struggling to

LEFT *German-allied Finnish soldiers. From left to right: lance-corporal, Finnish infantry, 1944; seargent, Finnish artillery, 1942; colonel, Finnish general staff, 1939. (Mike Chappell, from Men-at-Arms 131,* Germany's Eastern Front Allies 1941–45)

BELOW *Soviet troops at the defence of Brest fortress, 1941. From left to right: Red Army rifleman; lieutenant, NVKD Border Troops; Senior Battalion Kommisar, Red Army. Isolated by the German advance, with no hope of relief, the garrison of the fortress fought on until its ammunition was exhausted, an early indication that the Red Army might not be the easy opponent Hitler anticipated. (Ron Volstad, from Men-at-Arms 216,* The Red Army of the Great Patriotic War 1941–45)

EASTERN EUROPE AND THE USSR 1941

Hitler's war against the Soviet Union led to the largest armies ever maintained fighting the greatest land battles yet seen. The frontline would ultimately stretch for over 1,500 miles and at any one time there were close to ten million soldiers under arms. Note how the vast Pripyat marsh sits square in the path of an invader from the west. Partisan activity from 1942–44 would be concentrated in the swamps and forests shown here. Note also the pivotal importance of Moscow as the hub of the Soviet rail network.

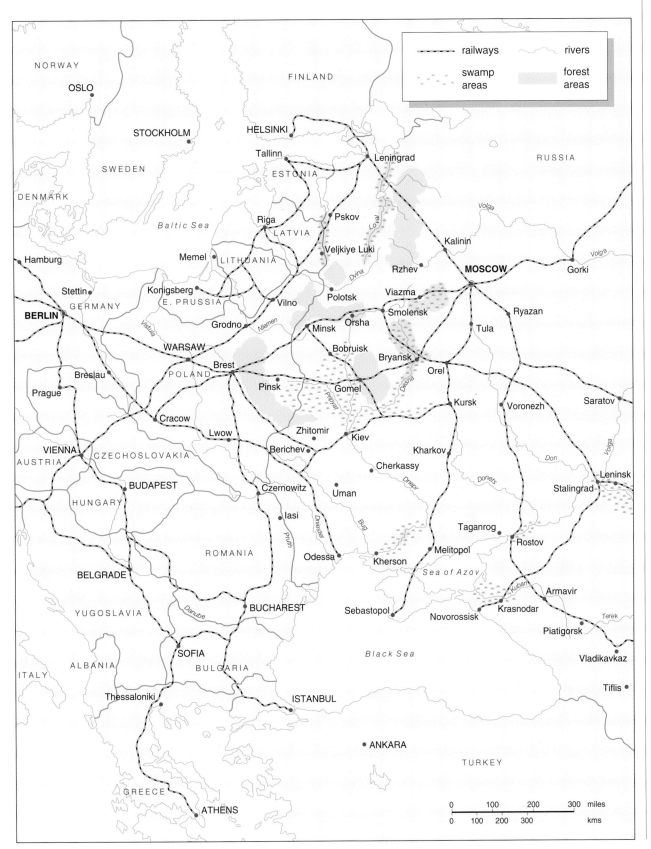

LEFT *Finnish soldiers with a captured Soviet OT-64 flame-thrower tank. The Red Army's invasion of Finland exposed many serious shortcomings, especially the inexperience of the officers who had risen to command in the wake of Stalin's purges. (IWM)*

BELOW LEFT *Finnish ski troops worked their way behind the advancing Russian columns north of Lake Ladoga, cutting the Russians' supply lines before chopping each column to pieces. (IWM)*

farm in Russia's unforgiving climate. Yet their determination to control the countryside, to abolish private farms and direct agricultural production from Moscow probably caused what they were seeking to prevent. The largely apolitical peasantry conceived a deep loathing for the regime. Resistance was passive: the productivity of collective farms would remain so bad for fifty years that even by the 1980s, the five per cent or so of privately-cultivated land (allowed after Stalin's death) supplied over a quarter of the USSR's food stocks. When the German forces invaded, they were welcomed as liberators across the Ukraine, and attempts by Moscow to create partisan movements across western Russia were sabotaged by the villagers who betrayed the guerrillas to the Germans. Their hopes were soon dashed of course, the invaders regarding them as *untermensch*, racial-inferiors to be exterminated or used for slave labour. As for abolishing collective farms, more than one Nazi observed that if collective farms had not been introduced, the Germans would have had to invent them. They were tailor-made feudal estates for the new German rulers.

The 'Bolshevik Old Guard', the original revolutionaries catapulted to power in 1917, knew a great deal about Stalin. The party cadres were not unanimously behind him either: nearly a quarter of them voted against him in what they foolishly thought was a secret ballot in 1934. Stalin had the old Bolsheviks arrested and shot and commenced a thorough purge of the Communist Party too. Of the 1,966 delegates to the 17th Party Congress, 1,108 had been arrested by the 18th Congress in 1939, by which time three quarters of the central committee elected in 1934 had also been shot.

Although a number of Soviet officers were arrested on trumped-up charges in the early 1930s, two institutions had so far largely escaped Stalin's terror - the armed forces and the instruments of terror themselves, the NKVD (the Russian acronym for 'Peoples' Commissariat of Internal Affairs'; previous titles for the communist secret police included Cheka and OGPU, later titles include MVD and KGB). Half-a-dozen generals were seized when the show trials of former leading communists Zinoviev and Kamenev began in 1936. The army's most senior advocate of mechanisation, Marshal Mikhail Tukachevsky, was demoted after increasingly public clashes with Stalin's civil war cronies Marshals Voroshilov and Budenny. In early 1937 Stalin moved against the NKVD, Commissar-General Yagoda was arrested along with some 3,000 of his officers. Yagoda himself was tried and executed with Party theorist Bukharin the following year. Tukachevsky was arrested in May 1937 and shot on 12 June, the firing squad commanded by his friend Marshal Blyukher (unaware his own death warrant was already signed on Stalin's desk).

In the days of the Tsars, national administration was remote, almost irrelevant compared to local concerns. Under Stalin, the hand of government could not be avoided. Industry had made its 'great leap forward', the entire rural economy re-shaped and the 'class struggle' kept to the fore – Stalin claimed it would intensify as the last surviving elements of capitalism fought to prevent the final victory of socialism. The ideological veneer was accepted by party activists, but society had been brutalised and life cheapened. Recent studies suggest western estimates of eleven million deaths in the 1930s should be revised to 16 or even 19 million. By the time the armed forces were purged in 1937 there were some seven million people held in remote labour camps, the GULAG.[10] Another seven or eight million people were herded off to the camps between 1937 and the German invasion. This total of 14–15 million people, representing about a tenth of the Soviet work force, provided slave labour in the mining and forestry industries across the bleak wilderness of Siberia. In the Vorkuta coal mines the temperature is below freezing for more than half the year. Prisoners worked outside at the Kolmya River gold mines in temperatures of -50°C. In such

conditions, less than ten per cent of the people arrested in the mid-1930s were still alive in 1941. Some camps were simply execution centres for political opponents: in the Baikal-Amur camps the NKVD resorted to mass shootings rather than wait for starvation or disease to eliminate the 'enemies of the people'.

No lists of these camps was ever published, the GULAG system never mentioned in the media, but everyone was aware of the threat, the possibility of being taken up on the way to work, or of the NKVD knocking on the apartment door in the small hours of the morning.

The system was also exported. Any potential focus for opposition to future Communist rule was eliminated in Soviet-occupied Poland in 1939 and the Baltic States in 1940. To be a teacher, political activist, trade union leader or military officer was enough to guarantee arrest. In a single night in June 1941, one week before the German invasion, the NKVD deported 132,000 people from Latvia, Lithuania and Estonia to the Russian interior. NKVD records from 1940 detail the removal of 15,031 Polish officers from prisoner-of-war camps where they had been held since September 1939. The same records make it clear these men never arrived in other camps. They disappeared. Not until 1989 did the Soviet government admit their fate, although one of the killing fields, at Katyn outside Smolensk, was unearthed by German troops in 1943. Mass graves there contained 4,000 bodies, all shot in the back of the head.

THE RED ARMY AT WAR 1939–40

The Nazi-Soviet Pact enabled Stalin to occupy the Baltic republics of Latvia, Lithuania and Estonia as well as eastern Poland. Finland, which achieved independence in 1917 (and extracted territorial concessions from the Bolsheviks during the Russian Civil War) was next. Stalin demanded that the border be moved 25 miles further away from Leningrad. His intention was to create a defensive zone as far to the west as possible, in readiness for the likely confrontation with Germany. When the Finns refused, Stalin ordered the troops of the Leningrad military district to teach them a lesson.

Although the Leningrad military district commanded the assault, divisions were despatched to the front from several other areas, often at short notice. Late November is not the best time to begin military operations in Finland, but in the atmosphere described above, no-one was going to object. Marshal Voroshilov assured Stalin that Red Army tanks would be driving through Helsinki within a week.

The Finns had fortified the Karelian isthmus and the crude tactical methods adopted by the Red Army failed utterly. To the north of Lake Ladoga, Russian divisions struggled along the few roads to be cut off by Finnish ski troops. The 44th Rifle Division (rushed up from Kiev) was surrounded, broken into remnants unable to

support each other, and annihilated. Newsreels showed roads choked with tanks and equipment, frozen corpses of Russian soldiers clustered around them. Between the slaughter in the snow and the desperate frontal attacks on the Mannerheim Line, the Red Army suffered some 200,000 casualties. Only weight of numbers enabled the Soviets to prevail. The Finns mobilised just about every able-bodied man to create an army about 600,000 strong but weak in artillery and supported by about 250 aircraft. The Soviets employed nearly a million men and by mid-January 1940 enough heavy guns and ammunition had been brought forward to commence a 16 day

ABOVE *A Soviet T-35 1935 model, belonging to 5th Independent Heavy Tank Brigade. Only 61 of these eleven-man 45-ton monsters were built. Most were lost to mechanical failure in the summer of 1941, but a handful survived to take part in the defence of Moscow. (Steven Zaloga)*

BELOW *Some of the lucky ones: over 1,000 Soviet troops of the 44th division surrendered at Suomussalmi. Their commander escaped from the encirclement but was shot by the NKVD. The price of failure in the Red Army would be equally high in 1941. (R. Tomasi)*

RIGHT *Italian soldiers examine the wreck of a BT-7 tank in 1941. The BT light tank series was developed from the designs of American engineer Walter Christie and were produced throughout the 1930s in Kharkov. (Author's collection)*

BELOW *A Soviet KV-1 1940 model, showing the up-armoured turret, in action in Leningrad in 1941. The slogan on the turret reads 'We defend the Conquests of October', a reference to the October 1917 revolution – just the sort of catchy phrase Marxist polemic was famous for. (Steven Zaloga)*

bombardment of the defences. The Red Army bludgeoned its way to Viipuri, despite heavy snowstorms in late February. An armistice was agreed on 13 March and the disputed territory incorporated into the USSR.

The Winter War seemed to confirm the German High Command's perception of the Red Army - an old-fashioned ponderous mass just like the army Germany had defeated in World War I. Its equipment was not impressive, the tanks deployed to Finland were either light tanks too vulnerable to anti-tank guns or super-heavy multi-turreted monsters that bogged down on remote forest tracks. Its officers had presided over

a shambles that would have discredited the Tsarist army of 1914 – or even 1905. Occurring just as Hitler was preparing his offensive in the west, the Red Army's performance in Finland suggested that it would be no match for the Wehrmacht.

Although Voroshilov was replaced as Defence Commissar by Marshal Timoshenko and political commissars in military units lost their role as 'co-commanders', the Winter War led neither to meaningful reforms nor to the end of the purges. The commission to review the battle tactics in Finland was chaired by a military Luddite, the ageing cavalry chief Marshal Budenny (described to Von Rundstedt in 1941 by a captured Russian officer as 'a man with a very large moustache but a very small brain'). Although the terror had slowed down, officers were still vanishing in the night to face charges of treason up to and beyond 22 June 1941.

Marshal Tukachevsky's remaining disciples managed to reverse an earlier decision to break up the mechanised corps and distribute tanks piece-meal among the infantry. Eight mechanised corps were authorised in the summer of 1940 and another 21 ordered in February 1941, but they would not be combat ready by the time of the invasion. However, even the new Chief of the General Staff, Georgi Zhukov, could not prevent Stalin ordering the disarming of the fortifications along the Russian border. Having obtained new buffer territories from Finland through the Baltic States, Poland and northern Romania, Stalin

insisted that defences be built along his new frontier, and the old positions – the 'Stalin Line' – were stripped to provide material and weapons for them. The Red Army ended up with two sets of incomplete fortifications. The decision to defend 'forward' had similar repercussions for the Soviet air arm. Air regiments were brought westward to primitive fields with no facilities or to civilian air strips. The German invasion caught a large proportion of front-line aircraft on the ground, jammed wing-tip to wing-tip, waiting for their new bases to be completed.

Zhukov owed his elevation to the one success of Stalin's Red Army; administering a comprehensive defeat to the Japanese in Manchuria. In the summer of 1938, border incidents between the Japanese and Soviets culminated in a small battle at Lake Khasan, about 70 miles from Vladivostock. The following spring, the Japanese Kwangtung army seized the village of Nomonhan on the remote border between Manchuria and Outer Mongolia, the River Khalkin-Gol. Zhukov masterminded a counter-attack, deploying some 60,000 troops and 500 tanks in a battle of encirclement which anticipated the larger scale battles of 1941–45. Soviet losses were about 23,000, Japanese casualties over 61,000. Japan made peace, and although major Soviet forces would remain to watch the border until Japan attacked Pearl Harbor, the Japanese army had lost its appetite for war with the USSR.

Promoted to command the Kiev military district, Zhukov worked energetically to repair the damage done by the purges. He emphasised that the Red Army would have to fight with what it had now, not what was due to come along in a year or two. In a wargame of a possible German invasion, he commanded the attackers and ran rings around his opponent General Pavlov. Appointed Chief-of-Staff in February 1941, he was so convinced of the inevitability of a Russo-German war that he urged Stalin to consider a pre-emptive strike.

Stalin would not hear of it, indeed he did everything possible to avert an invasion, ordering anti-aircraft units not to fire on the increasingly blatant over-flights by German reconnaissance aircraft. Deliveries of strategic materials to Germany, one of the key features of the Nazi-Soviet Pact were maintained so rigorously that several trainloads passed from east to west only hours before the German attack. The Pact gained Germany 1,000,000 tons of feed grains, 900,000 tons of gasoline, 500,000 tons of phosphates and 100,000 tons of chromium ores. Permission to import raw materials from Iran, Romania and the Far East via the USSR was also granted and exploited. Stalin calculated that if he gave Hitler no provocation, the war could be delayed until Soviet forces were properly prepared. As it became obvious that Hitler planned to invade anyway, and every indication pointed to an invasion in the summer of 1941, Stalin still refused to take the necessary steps to prepare his forces on the frontier. However, there is evidence that a highly secret committee reporting to Stalin was already thinking the unthinkable. It worked on the assumption not just that the Germans would invade, but that their forces would be able to advance deep into Russia before the Red Army could do anything about it.[11]

CHAPTER THREE

TO THE GATES OF MOSCOW

'Before three months have passed, we shall witness a collapse in Russia, the like of which has never been seen in history'

Adolf Hitler, 22 June 1941

The German invasion forces were divided into three Army Groups. Commanded by General von Leeb, Army Group North was to advance from East Prussia, through the Baltic States and on to Leningrad. Detaching several divisions to besiege the border fortress of Brest-Litovsk, General von Bock's Army Group Centre was to pass north of the Pripyat marshes, heading for Minsk, Smolensk and ultimately Moscow. Field Marshal von Rundstedt's Army Group South occupied a start line that arced from southern Poland, along the Hungarian frontier and across Romania. Ahead lay the great plains of southern Russia and the Ukraine – excellent tank country.

While each Group had broad territorial objectives, the German armies had not come to conquer cities. They were there to kill Russians. Hitler and the General Staff were in complete agreement, the Soviet forces had to be trapped and beaten in European Russia, preferably within 250 miles of the border. Their concern was that the Soviets might fall back deep into the Russian interior, drawing German forces into a battle of attrition on the edge of Asia. The German strategy looked perfectly orthodox, following the precepts laid down by Von Clausewitz. The great nineteenth century strategist had argued that the capture of great cities was rarely decisive, but if the enemy's army was destroyed, his capital would fall automatically; therefore make the army the primary objective. In fact the German high command had no choice in the matter. An invasion on such a scale presented immense logistical problems. Logistics dictated only one strategy, and there would be only one chance to make it work.

The Soviet equivalent of an Army Group was a 'Front', four of which were deployed from Finland to Romania. The North Front, commanded by Colonel-general Popov, was the smallest: it faced the Finns and the German army in Norway. The North-West Front under Colonel-general Kuznetsov defended the Baltic States, while General Pavlov's Western Front faced Army Group Centre. Colonel-general Kirponos' South-West Front held the line from southern Poland and along the Hungarian border. Armies deployed opposite Romania were organised into a

RIGHT *A Panzer III of 1st Panzergruppe advances across the northern Ukraine, July 1941. The German tank commanders were rather proprietorial, both Guderian and Von Kleist marking their vehicles with their initial. (Author's collection)*

fifth Front, the Southern, under General Tiulenev a few days after the invasion. The Soviet high command, Stavka,[12] was also assembling reserve armies between Moscow and Smolensk.

Each German invasion since 1939 had opened with a devastating air attack, and the Luftwaffe showed it had lost nothing of its edge despite the losses over Britain and Greece. Over-flights before the attack had provided a good intelligence picture of the Soviet air forces and on 22 June the 66 air bases that were home to about three-quarters of Soviet aircraft were systematically bombed. About 800 Soviet aircraft were destroyed on the ground, while another 400 were shot down in some very one-sided air battles. The Luftwaffe had better fighters and many veteran pilots who soon ran up enormous personal 'scores'.

The Luftwaffe had so many targets in the opening months of Barbarossa it could not bomb them all. So many columns of Russian troops were spotted moving behind the front that many had to be ignored while more pressing targets were dealt with. There was, incredibly, a shortage of bombs – a combination of inadequate production with sloppy logistic planning. The plethora of targets and the army's escalating demand for close air support ruled out any serious strategic effort by the Luftwaffe in 1941. Indeed, the army began to rely more and more on airpower to compensate for its own problems. The vigorous presence of the Luftwaffe over the Russian battlefields was not the manifestation of German technical superiority it seemed at the time. It was a symptom of the army's weaknesses, its lack of artillery, anti-tank weapons and the fact that only a small proportion of the army was mechanised. The Panzer forma-

tions depended on air support both to break through the Soviet defences and to hold the 'outer ring' of the lines of encirclement that they found themselves holding.[13] The Panzers needed bombers to compensate for their relative lack of organic artillery (and shells) as well as transports to deliver emergency supplies of POL and ammunition. It was fortunate for the German army that the Luftwaffe won air supremacy so quickly, wiping out the Soviet air force and freeing its assets for support of the ground war.

The massacre in the air was immediately followed by one on land. The Soviet forces were caught completely unprepared, Stalin's absolute insistence on offering no 'provocation' had left them in no position to offer effective resistance. When an incredulous Stalin finally accepted the news was true, that Hitler had broken his word and invaded, he demanded a counter-attack.

OPERATION BARBAROSSA 1941

The initial pace of the German advance exceeded their wildest expectations. By August it even seemed possible that Russia might be beaten in the eight weeks, as Hitler predicted. The Baltic States and Belorussia fell quickly, the Ukraine next and over a million Soviet troops were taken prisoner. Yet by the time the German advance ground to a halt outside Moscow, the German army had suffered 750,000 casualties.

LEFT *The German army consisted of a relatively small mechanised force and a much larger body still dependent on horse-drawn transport. Here, in a scene which could be from the American Civil War, elements of Army Group North press on to catch up with the Panzers. (R. Tomasi)*

BELOW LEFT *Troops from Army Group North during their rapid advance across the Baltic States. As the Soviets withdrew, the NKVD executed hundreds of political prisoners. In some towns, there were local uprisings against the regime as the German forces approached. (IWM)*

Marshal Timoshenko wrote the orders and issued them that very night. All four Fronts were to launch an immediate offensive, but were not to pursue beyond the 1941 border! All commanders attempted to comply, putting in at least a token counter-strike while trying to salvage something from the mess, but none managed to arrest the ferocious pace of the German assault.

BATTLES OF ENCIRCLEMENT

The German Army Groups advanced in two echelons; the Panzer divisions and motorised divisions grouped together into four Panzer Groups, one each in the north and south and two for Army Group Centre. The Panzer Groups cut through the front line and pressed on, trapping the Russian armies between them and the mass of infantry divisions hurrying forward in their wake. There would be no supply line to the Panzer Groups, shuttling supplies forward would be impossible with so many unsubdued enemy formations in between. Each Panzer division therefore carried about twice its normal allocation of fuel.[14]

Army Group Centre's Panzer Groups drove 200 miles in five days, reaching Minsk in a pincer movement that cut off most of the Russian 3rd, 10th and 13th Armies. Pavlov's western front was torn apart. Isolated units and thousands of stragglers managed to slip away before the hard-marching German infantry sealed the pocket, but a staggering 350,000 prisoners were taken, along with 2,500 tanks and 1,400 guns.

Army Group North was the smallest of the German groups, but it had the easiest task initially because the road network in the Baltic States and Belorussia was more extensive than in the regions south of the Pripyat. In a matter of days, the Panzer divisions were through Lithuania and halfway across Latvia, reaching the River Dvina on 26 June. Soviet mechanised units found themselves out of contact with the high command or adjacent units, and out of ammunition and fuel shortly afterwards.

In the south, Field Marshal von Rundstedt encountered more determined opposition, as General Kirponos committed his mechanised forces to counter-attack. A handful of T-34s made their first terrifying appearance on 23 June, the anti-tank teams of the German 197th Infantry Division discovering to their dismay that their 37mm anti-tank guns made no impression on them. General von Kleist's 1st Panzer Group faced several major counter-attacks by Soviet armour, but experience told – the veteran German units co-ordinated their actions while their opponents often blundered into battle, unsupported by neighbouring formations. The Luftwaffe had achieved complete air superiority and concentrations of Soviet troops were bombed from the moment they tried to assemble.

Army Group Centre made faster progress than Army Group South, reaching Smolensk by 26 July. The rapid exhaustion of both fuel and ammunition as well as stiffening Soviet resistance on the high road to Moscow would prevent any further advance for the moment. Meanwhile a large salient was appearing around Kiev, as German forces swept across the southern Ukraine. Stalin insisted that General Kirponos' South-West Front continue to counter-attack, sacking his old crony Marshal Budenny for supporting Kirponos' plea for permission to retreat. Both sides could read a map, and Hitler responded to the invitation by ordering Guderian's 2nd Panzer Group (part of Army Group Centre) to drive south from the Smolensk area. Army Group South's 1st Panzer Group headed up from Kremenchug on the River Dnepr. On 16 September, the armoured pincers met, trapping four Soviet armies totalling nearly 50 divisions. The next day Stalin signalled permission to give up Kiev, but still said nothing about withdrawal. Possibly on his own initiative Marshal Timoshenko sent Major-general Ivan Bagramyan to Kirponos' headquarters with oral instructions to break out.

There was a fleeting chance of escape for those formations near the edge of the pocket, or those with commanders prepared to take decisions without reference to higher headquarters. As the German infantry divisions hurried to seal every avenue of escape, several key figures broke out including General Andrei Vlasov and Bagramyan. Kirponos led his staff out on foot but stepped on a mine and was killed. According to Soviet figures, the South-West Front had 677,000 men in late August, of which 150,000 escaped and 527,000 became prisoners-of-war. The more usually quoted German figure is 655,000 prisoners, a total possibly inflated by the many civilians dragged off to their deaths by the German army at the same time. Less than one in six of these prisoners would survive the year.

PRISONERS-OF-WAR
AND 'THE JEWISH PROBLEM'

Kiev fell on 19 September. A few days later an order printed in Ukrainian and Russian was posted throughout the town by the occupation forces. It read:

'Jews of the city of Kiev and surroundings: on Monday September 29, you are to appear by 7.00 a.m. with your possessions, money, documents, valuables, and warm clothing at Dorogozhitshaya Street, next to the Jewish Cemetery. Failure to appear is punishable by death'.

No-one realised just what the Germans had in store, that the warm clothing would only be needed for a short walk from the trucks since everyone would have to strip naked before stepping into the pits to be shot. In 48 hours, the SS men of Sonderkommando 4a and two kommandos of Police Regiment South shot 33,771 Jews in a nearby ravine at Babi Yar. Fooled until the last moment, the victims were made to lie on the still-warm bodies at the top of the heap, before the guards opened fire with sub-machine guns and pistols. Although the bodies were bayoneted too, to check no-one had been missed, a few individuals escaped death, lying under other bodies until they could slip away at night.

Four Einsatzgruppen entered the USSR in the wake of the German army. These 3,000 SS men were to provide internal security by combating Soviet partisan activity, but their primary purpose was to kill the Jewish population of eastern Europe. Since 90 per cent of Soviet Jews lived in towns, this was quickly accomplished, and 1.5 million people were put to death. The Einsatzgruppen had enormous impact on the

War in the East, their strength growing tenfold during 1941. By the beginning of 1943 there were 300,000 men engaged in their genocidal mission – this at a time when the German army was desperately under strength. The zeal with which the Einsatzgruppen dealt with the least hint of resistance behind the lines won them plaudits from every army headquarters. However, some junior army officers refused to co-operate with SS men who combed the prisoner-of-war camps for Jewish members of the Soviet armed forces. The Commandant of a POW camp at Vinnitsa even court martialled his deputy for handing over POWs to the SS, but the Army High Command issued a formal instruction that soldiers were to assist the Einsatzgruppen. 'This order clearly states that the Wehrmacht has to co-operate in the solution of this problem.'[15] Some army units were already complying with a will. The soldiers and junior NCOs had grown up under Hitler and had no reservations about their mission in Russia. A significant minority – 29 per cent in one analysis of three front-line Wehrmacht divisions – were Nazi Party members.[16]

The Army High Command was already sliding down the moral slope, issuing the notorious 'Commissar order' before the invasion. Soviet political officers who were captured were to be shot immediately. An OKH order of 6 May also authorised retaliation ('corrective measures') against villages in the vicinity of any partisan resistance. Worse, the order specifically exempted soldiers from the legal code for a whole catalogue of crimes – German troops literally had a license to kill.

The German army's reaction to the vast quan-

ABOVE *Although some pockets of resistance (such as the garrison of Brest-Litovsk) fought with exceptional courage, Soviet soldiers surrendered in enormous numbers in the summer of 1941. (Author's collection)*

ABOVE LEFT *German security troops, 1941–42. From left to right: leutnant, Galician Police, Poland; wachtmeister, German Schutzpolizei Battalion; SS-Untersturmführer, SD-Einsatzgruppe. Locally-recruited security forces assisted the SD in its work, executing Communist officials out of hand and combing the prisoner-of-war camps for Jews. Any found were shot. (Mike Chappell, from Men-at-Arms 142, Partisan Warfare 1941–45)*

RIGHT *A PzKpfw IV Ausf.F of 11.Pz.-Div. in action in south Russia, 1941. The letter 'K' denotes the division belongs to Panzergruppe Kleist. The 60-year old former cavalry general proved one of the most able tank commanders of the war and was promoted to Field Marshal in January 1943. He died in Soviet captivity in 1954. (David Smith)*

BELOW RIGHT *A mass of Soviet transport vehicles clogs the roads out of Kiev as German bombers swoop to attack. Colonel-general Kirponos was ordered to hold the Kiev area by Stalin, condemning him and over 500,000 soldiers to their deaths.*

tities of prisoners was in the same spirit: on 8 September 1941 OKH decreed that Soviet POWs had forfeited all rights and that any measures were permissible. By then, nearly two million Soviet servicemen had been captured and winter was approaching. No provision had been made to deal with so many prisoners and on receipt of this order many army units simply machine-gunned their captives. The majority were left in barbed-wire compounds, deprived of food and warm clothing and allowed to starve or freeze to death in conditions of indescribable squalor. The only regret ever expressed by the Nazi leadership was that this was a waste of potential slave labour, Alfred Rosenberg writing to Field Marshal Keitel in February 1942;

'The fate of the Soviet prisoners-of-war in Germany is on the contrary a tragedy of the greatest extent. Of the 3.6 million prisoners-of-war, only several hundred thousand are still able to work fully. A large part of them has starved or died because of the hazards of the weather. Thousands also died from spotted fever. The camp commanders have forbidden the civilian population to put food at the disposal of the prisoners, and they have rather let them starve to death'.[17]

The military repercussions of German savagery would not be felt immediately, not until news of their crimes spread throughout a Russia that was no stranger to arbitrary cruelty. Despite their actions, the Germans managed to recruit several million Russians and other nationalities to fight for them in the east. How many more would have rallied to them had more humane treatment been

offered has been debated ever since the war. Since the NKVD was still dealing with the burning embers of Ukrainian nationalism in the early 1950s, opposition to the Soviet regime was clearly widespread. The Germans' evil crimes rebounded on them and arguably cost them the war.

The mass surrenders of 1941 suggested that large elements of the Red Army were no more ready to die for their country than those of France in 1940 or the Italian army in North Africa where

300,000 men surrendered to 30,000 British and Commonwealth soldiers. There was no folk memory of atrocity. Fraternisation between German and Russian soldiers had been as common on the eastern front during World War I as on the western front. Easter 1916 had witnessed scenes not dissimilar to those of the notorious unofficial Christmas truce on the western front in 1914. Suspicious that his armies would continue to disintegrate, Stalin ordered NKVD chief Lavrenti Beria to restore discipline. Before the men of the Red Army learned what an appalling fate was in store for anyone surrendering to the Germans, Beria had already made surrender a crime, punishable in the NKVD's usual way. Officers and political officials who had been taken prisoner were declared traitors, and their families made to suffer for their 'crime'. This had tragic consequences for many men who held out behind the lines, fought their way back and found themselves in the hands of the NKVD, branded as 'enemies of the people'.

Stalin had the unfortunate General Pavlov and his staff arrested as traitors. The officers were tortured into confessing that they were part of a German plot and had betrayed their men at the battle of Minsk. Stalin had his scapegoats for the disaster, but to announce that a Front headquarters had been unmasked as a nest of traitors was hardly calculated to boost morale in the rest of the army.

MUD, ICE AND THE ROAD TO MOSCOW
German objectives changed during September. Although the German army had inflicted enormous losses on the Red Army, Soviet resistance was continuing and the German forces running out of supplies and replacements. The initial progress in the North had petered to a halt in the dense forests and swamps that barred the approaches to Leningrad. The terrain was unsuited to armoured operations and the 4th Panzer Group – poised at one stage for a mad solo dash at the city – was reassigned to Army Group Centre. Deprived of its tanks, Army Group North ground its way to the outskirts of Leningrad in fighting more akin to World War I than the brave new world of Blitzkrieg.

The Red Army had suffered grievously, but was still in the field. On 6 September Hitler demanded a maximum effort to capture Moscow before winter set in. The Soviet capital was at once a political and military objective. It was hoped that the loss of the city and the Kremlin would demoralise the Red Army if not unseat the Soviet regime. Moscow was also a key industrial centre and lay at the hub of the Soviet rail network.

TOP LEFT *Smolensk smoulders following its fall on 5 August. However, Army Group Centre outran its supply lines here. In August General Zhukov led an attack at Jel'n'a, 75km south-east, badly mauling the German 20th Corps. (Author's collection)*

TOP RIGHT *German infantry follow a Sturmgeschütz battery towards Kiev. Eight battalions of StuGs and six independent batteries took part in the initial stages of Barbarossa. (Author's collection)*

ABOVE RIGHT *German infantry dismount from SdKfz 251 half-tracks, the standard armoured personnel carrier of the Panzer divisions. However, only one battalion in each regiment had them: the others had to make do with trucks. (US National Archives)*

BELOW RIGHT *The battle for Narva, September 1941. In ten weeks, Army Group North had conquered the Baltic States and was within 100km of Leningrad. (R. Tomasi)*

CENTRE *Norwegian, Danish and Dutch volunteers made up about a third of the 5th SS division Wiking in 1941; a proportion that would increase during the war. Wiking was part of Army Group South, and fought as far as Rostov, from which it had to withdraw during the Soviet winter offensive. (Author's collection)*

BOTTOM *The great battles of encirclement in 1941 led to some 3.6 million Soviet soldiers passing into captivity. Deprived of food, warm clothing, and medical care, they were deliberately starved to death that winter: more than 75 per cent were dead by early 1942. (Author's collection)*

Political considerations aside, its loss would hamper Soviet strategic movement, logistic arrangements and military production. As usual, the Germans planned to isolate the city rather than embroil themselves in an urban battle: 3rd and 4th Panzer Groups were to bypass Moscow to the north, the 2nd Panzer Group would advance from Tula, passing to the south and linking up with the others some distance east of Moscow.

Operation 'Typhoon' opened on 2 October, and led immediately to two more battles of encirclement. Another 650,000 Red Army soldiers passed into captivity. With the 2nd, 3rd and 4th Panzer Groups concentrated in Army Group Centre, the Wehrmacht was staking everything on its dwindling mechanised units. The three Groups consisted of a total of 13 Panzer divisions and seven motorised divisions, although the total tank strength was probably no more than 1,000. By this time, most motorised formations had lost over half their vehicles. For example, in three months of fighting, 2nd Panzer Group had advanced across some 1,200 miles of Soviet territory: since the Germans calculated that for every mile 'conquered' combat vehicles actually drove two miles, the wear and tear on vehicles (not to mention crews) was depleting the tank regiments as fast as actual battle. Nevertheless, the Panzer Groups advanced rapidly, cutting off the 19th, 20th, 24th and 32nd Soviet armies at Vyazma. The 13th and 50th armies were encircled as the 2nd Panzer Group broke through to Orel.

There was panic in Moscow. Party functionaries raced to pack their bags as the regime implemented its emergency plan to transfer most government departments to Kuibyshev, 600 miles away. Alexander Werth, the British correspondent in Moscow observed the stampede to the east on 16 October, and how it suddenly stopped when it was announced that Stalin would be staying in the Kremlin.

Three factors helped him decide to stand in the path of the Panzers. The first light fall of snow dusted German positions on the night of 6 October, heralding not the iron grip of winter, but the autumn rains that turned the roads into a sticky morass. Russians call this time of year the *rasputitsa* – the 'time without roads', and it would impose a temporary halt to operations every year, along with its counterpart the *bezdororzh'e*, the spring thaw. Stalin could always count on the mud, but in October 1941 he could also count on the Japanese. Some 750,000 Soviet troops were stationed in the Far East, in case the Japanese generals planned further aggression there. Now Soviet intelligence sources in Japan confirmed that the Tojo government intended to launch a war against the United States. And it was now too late in the year for Japan to contemplate an attack on the USSR. By mid-November some ten divisions were sent to the Moscow front from Siberia and Central Asia. Although there was no mass transfer of units from the Far East, the Red Army in Manchuria supplied a steady stream of replacements to the formations around the capital.

The third reason for Stalin's confidence was the staggering success with which the Red Army mobilisation system was creating new divisions. The GUF (Reserve Armies Administration), established in July oversaw a massive expansion of the Red Army that compensated for the terrible losses of the summer campaign. Between July and 1 December 1941 the Red Army mobilised 143 new rifle divisions and replaced 84 rifle divisions

that had been destroyed in combat. The Moscow military district was the greatest source of recruits, supplying 26 divisions, possibly because its manpower reserves were swollen by refugees and stragglers.[18]

Although the fighting on the approaches to Moscow was at its height by then, the issue delicately balanced, Stavka held its nerve and refused to commit the powerful reserves it had assembled. Instead, the fresh troops were held in readiness for a counter-attack.

On 7 November the first hard frost occurred, and the liquid mud solidified. It was also the day that the Soviet regime traditionally held a military parade through Red Square. The central committee was astonished when Stalin calmly announced his intention to hold the parade as usual, despite the proximity of the front line and the obvious threat of air attack. It was a timely display of confidence. Stalin was scenting victory even as German reconnaissance patrols were approaching the outlying stations of the Moscow metro.

LEFT *Latvian and Ukranian volunteers, 1941–43. From left to right: korporal, Ukranian 'Schuma' battalion; virsserzants, Latvian 'Schuma'; korporal, Ukranian 'Schuma'. (Mike Chappell, from Men-at-Arms 142,* Partisan Warfare 1941–45*)*

BELOW *Soviet troops at the defence of Leningrad, 1941–42. From left to right: sergeant, Red Army Rifle Forces; lieutenant, Red Army Medical Branch; naval infantryman, Baltic fleet. (Ron Volstad, from Men-at-Arms 216,* The Red Army of the Great Patriotic War 1941–45*)*

THE SUMS THAT NEVER WORKED

Directly the ground hardened, the German advance resumed. In the South, Von Kleist's 1st Panzer Group approached Rostov and Von Manstein's newly-formed 11th Army swept into the Crimea, driving the Russians back on the great naval base at Sevastopol. The new industrial city of Kharkov and the whole Donbass region, economic powerhouse of the USSR, was overrun. Despite the increasing cold, daytime temperatures averaging –5°C, and its severely depleted units, Army Group Centre battered its way towards Moscow. On 28 November, elements of the 7th Panzer Division forced a crossing over the Moscow–Volga canal. Some troops were within 12 miles or so of the city, and in the cold clear air, the distant spires were visible through binoculars. Their reports generated great excitement at Hitler's headquarters, but few officers on the ground still believed they would enter the city. Unit strengths were dwindling at an alarming rate, there were no replacements, and the Red Army was contesting every yard of ground with tremendous bravery and increasing military competence. And supplies were running out.

Most front-line soldiers affect a disdain for the supply services, the REMFs whose dull duty it is to forward the gasoline, ammunition, rations and

ABOVE *Soviet troops from the defence of Moscow, 1941–42. From left to right: sergeant-major, Red Army Rifle Forces; Red Army rifleman; tank crewman, 1st Moscow Motorised Rifle Division. Note the dog carrying an explosive charge. Trained to run under German vehicles, these canine kamikazes were introduced in late 1941 and were still being encountered as late as summer 1943. German soldiers tended to shoot dogs on sight. (Ron Volstad, from* Men-at-Arms 216, The Red Army of the Great Patriotic War 1941–45*)*

RIGHT *The T-34 came as a disagreeable surprise to the German army. It was all but immune to the standard 37mm anti-tank gun (seen here) and its 76mm gun could destroy any German tank it met. (IWM)*

surprise nor cause for alarm, even if some Panzer divisions only survived Soviet counter-attacks because emergency supplies of ammunition were flown in by air. What none of the soldiers standing at the gates of Moscow realised was that they were only there by a miracle, and it could not be sustained for much longer.

The entire invasion had been conducted on a logistic con trick. As we have seen, the Wehrmacht consisted of a relatively small mechanised army and a largely unmodernised force of infantry divisions. Although only part of the army's total strength was motorised, its demand for supplies, especially POL (petrol, oil, lubricants) created a heavier logistic burden than the armies of 1914–18. Unfortunately for the Wehrmacht, the German railway network had deteriorated since World War I: there were fewer locomotives and less rolling stock than in 1914. As the army moved deeper into Russia it would depend on the Russian rail network, which (as known from World War I) was built on a wide gauge incompatible with German rolling stock. The tracks could not carry as heavy a load as equivalent German ones. Even when the rails were converted to German gauge, all facilities like water towers were built for Russian engines and were too far apart for German engines. The latter were unsuited to the east anyway: their water tubes froze in the much colder winter temperatures and most of those sent to the USSR during the winter of 1941 became immobilised.

sundry necessities for the fighting men to do what they are paid for. So the rapid breakdown of German supply arrangements during the invasion of Russia caused great irritation and the usual flurry of angry signals. But it was neither a

RIGHT *The 1st and 4th Romanian Mountain Brigades fought in the Crimea under command of the German 11th Army (Von Manstein) in the winter of 1941–42. The Soviets counter-attacked on 30 December, establishing a bridgehead at Feodosiya. (R. Tomasi)*

BELOW RIGHT *Dead SS men in a possibly posed shot taken in the wake of the Soviet counter-attack outside Moscow. Hitler's greatest gamble had failed: the Soviet Union did not fall to a single campaign and Germany was now locked in a battle of attrition. Hitler's decision to declare war on the USA at this point simply beggars belief. (Tass)*

Neither could supplies be brought forward by truck. Even the mechanised formations had no spare vehicles to shuttle back and forth between rail heads: they needed every truck they had. To obtain enough trucks, the German army had seized vehicles from all over Europe because German industry was only delivering a fraction of the quantities required.[19] In 1941 the Germans had more than 2,000 different vehicles in service, few sharing any common parts, and the situation never improved. For instance, in mid-1943 I Flak Corps had 260 different types of German vehicle on its strength and 120 different types of foreign vehicle. In many cases the Corps had just a couple of each type.

The roads were even worse than OKH planners had assumed and total fuel consumption rose to 330,000 tons per month, rather than the 250,000 budgeted for. Germany only had two or three months' supply of oil in reserve and it was discovered that captured Soviet petrol was unsuited to German engines.

The army's head quartermaster, Generalmajor Friedrich Paulus conducted a wargame in December 1940 which demonstrated that the logistic arrangements would collapse before the Germans reached the upper Dnepr. However, as the date for the offensive drew nearer, the famously professional German planners fudged the logistic plan again and again, persuading themselves that if the army could not sustain a campaign on this scale for six months, then the war would have to be won in three. Martin van Creveld's study of the 1941 campaign observes,

'the German General Staff seemed to have abandoned rational thought at this point'.[20]

December 1941 found the German army tantalisingly close to Moscow, but with no prospect of advancing further. Outside the capital the thermometer sank to an average –12°C every day, although plunging to –20° on occasion. Without winter clothing the soldiers froze, over 100,000

frostbite casualties were reported that month. Without winter equipment, heaters, special oils and lubricants, tanks and aircraft ceased to function too. Such was the chaos at the railheads far to the west, that even had the army possessed adequate quantities of cold-weather gear, it is unlikely it could have been brought forward.

On 5 December the Red Army counter-attacked. The temperature that day peaked at -15°C and the snow was about a metre deep. The German army had little air support: the Luftwaffe found it was taking five hours to get a bomber airborne in these conditions, and in any case, German aerial fuses did not function in snow that deep. The bombs just vanished into the snow without detonating. The Red Army placed greater reliance on artillery than aircraft, and its heavy guns and Katyusha rocket launchers functioned without apparent difficulty. Once driven out of their positions, the Germans found it impossible

ABOVE *Luftwaffe field division troops, 1941–42. From left to right: gefreiter, Luftwaffe Alarmeinheit; jäger, III.Feldregiment der Luftwaffe Nr.1; flieger, Fliegerhorst Yukhnov. (Ron Volstad, from Men-at-Arms 229,* Luftwaffe Field Divisions 1941–45*)*

TOP RIGHT *Romanian volunteers in Russia, 1941–43. From left to right: private 1st class, 13th Infantry Division; lieutenant, 10th Infantry Division; lieutenant-colonel, 7th Mountain Rifle Bn.(Horia Serbanescu, from Men-at-Arms 246,* The Romanian Army of World War II*)*

ABOVE RIGHT *LTvz38 of the 11th Tank Co., Slovak Mobile Division, Russia 1941. (Terry Hadler, from New Vanguard 26,* German Light Panzers 1932–42*)*

to dig new trenches in the frozen ground. Night-time temperatures were so cold that even the smallest villages assumed tactical importance. The dilemma was whether to try and survive in the open or seek shelter in a village that was likely to be on the Russian gunners' maps too.

Hitler had already sacked one of his most senior commanders. Army Group South was as over-extended as the forces before Moscow, and Field Marshal von Rundstedt had authorised 1st SS Division LSSAH to withdraw from Rostov at the end of November. When the Field Marshal said he would sooner resign than countermand a correct military decision, Hitler accepted his departure. On 18 December, the commander of Army Group Centre, General von Bock, was relieved of his command on 'health grounds' after arguing that his men should retreat to more defensible ground. Hitler then sacked the OKH chief-of-staff Field Marshal von Brauchitsch and appointed himself commander-in-chief instead. Even Hitler's earlier favourites were not spared. Heinz Guderian's 2nd Panzer Army tried to fall back too, and after a bitter interview at Rastenburg he was fired. His fellow Panzer General Höpner and Field Marshal von Leeb lost their commands too.

Hitler's gamble had failed. The Red Army had not collapsed, Moscow had not fallen and now his generals wanted to retreat. Where to? Drawing on his own personal experience of the western front in World War I, and arguing that it would be just as cold 50, 100 or even 200km west of Moscow, the Führer demanded that his soldiers stand fast. That they ultimately managed to stop the Red Army that winter, and went on to smash a major Russian offensive early in the spring, seemed to vindicate Hitler. Just as his insistence on the Ardennes strategy in 1940 had delivered victory, so his instinctive strategy in 1941 had triumphed despite the generals' objections. The Führer's confidence never wavered. In the wake of Japan's attack on Pearl Harbor, he declared war on the USA.

CHAPTER FOUR

ATTACK AND COUNTER-ATTACK

'We still need to assimilate the experience of modern war ...
neither here, nor today will the outcome of the war be decided. The crisis is yet far off' [21]

Marshal Shaposhnikov, December 1941

The dramatic reversal of fortunes at the gates of Moscow led Stalin to make the same premature assumption of victory that Hitler and his generals had been led to by the great battles of encirclement in the summer of 1941. No matter that Zhukov had husbanded the newly-mobilised (and only half-trained) reserves to make the Moscow counter-attack possible, that he had been supported by the majority of the Red air force, and the Germans had been at the extreme end of their tenuous supply lines. Stalin ordered immediate offensives all along the line from Leningrad to the Crimea.

The northern offensive failed. The front was temporarily ruptured, but the Red Army lacked the numerical superiority it had enjoyed on the Moscow front. And in place of Zhukov's ruthless energy, the commander was an NKVD political officer. The Germans managed to contain the attacking 2nd Shock Army and seal the front behind it. Some nine Soviet divisions remained

cut-off despite the appointment of General Vlasov to command them, and after nearly six months in isolation, the survivors surrendered in June 1942.

The German blockade of Leningrad continued. There was little thought of storming the city, merely bombing and shelling it and allowing the sub-zero temperatures and lack of food to do the rest. Hitler had publicly stated his intention to level the place. Although the famous

ABOVE *A T-34 and T-26 with Soviet ski-troops in early 1942. Stalin laid down insanely ambitious objectives for the Soviet winter offensive, but although the Red Army failed to achieve them, it had inflicted over 750,000 casualties on the Germans by this time. (IWM)*

LEFT *A KV-1 heavy tank makes a suitably spectac-ular exit from a forest. In early 1942 Soviet tank brigades had a company each of KV-1s, T-34s and T-40/60 light tanks. This did not work, and the formidable KV-1s were concentrated in discrete brigades from June onwards. (Author's collection)*

railway across the ice brought in some supplies over the frozen Lake Ladoga, hunger turned into starvation in the winter of 1941–2 and over half a million people perished. The bodies could not be buried and the city's sanitary system broke down. Only the intense cold prevented an epidemic. The stubborn, determined resistance of Leningrad is little known in the west, and Stalin, who pointedly never visited the city afterwards, took care it was not even commemorated in the USSR. The siege would eventually last for 900 days, but Stalin's response to this epic defence was to purge the Leningrad party after the war, possibly assassinating the former party boss Andrei Zhdanov in 1948 and removing senior figures (Kuznetzov, Kosygin and Voznesensky) associated with him and Leningrad.

In the Moscow area, the temperature sank to -25°C in January. The Kalinin and Western Fronts were ordered to destroy Army Group Centre, and came desperately close to doing so. The Germans reeled back, and before a coherent front line could be re-established, Russian cavalry units had penetrated far behind the lines, where they would remain a threat to German communications until the spring. Two Soviet armies, the 29th and 33rd, were cut off by German counter-attacks, forming pockets that were slowly reduced as better weather enabled German armour and aircraft to operate again.

In the harsh weather conditions, neither side managed to mount effective air attacks. The Luftwaffe had failed to seriously interrupt the evacuation of Soviet industries out of reach of German attack: the army's demand for close air support was unceasing and left no opportunity for strategic air missions. True, Moscow was attacked in the summer, beginning with a major raid on the

night of 21 July, when 127 bombers delivered 104 tons of bombs on the Soviet capital. But this was in part a reaction to the token bomber raid made on Berlin by 18 Ilyushin Il-4s of the Baltic Red Banner Fleet's torpedo/mine air wing on 6 August. The German raids on Moscow prompted more bombing by the Soviet long range air force in September, but the advance of the Ostheer soon put most airfields beyond range of Berlin. The

The Soviet counter-attack at the gates of Moscow was expanded by Stalin who demanded offensives along the whole front. In the north, the Soviet breakthrough was sealed off, encircling more Soviet armies. In the south great progress was made, the recapture of Rostov leading Hitler to sack Field Marshal von Rundstedt. Hitler chose the Ukraine for his offensive in 1942: it was excellent tank country and he now selected the Caucasus and the Soviet oil fields as his objective. Meanwhile, the 6th Army was drawn into a battle of attrition at Stalingrad.

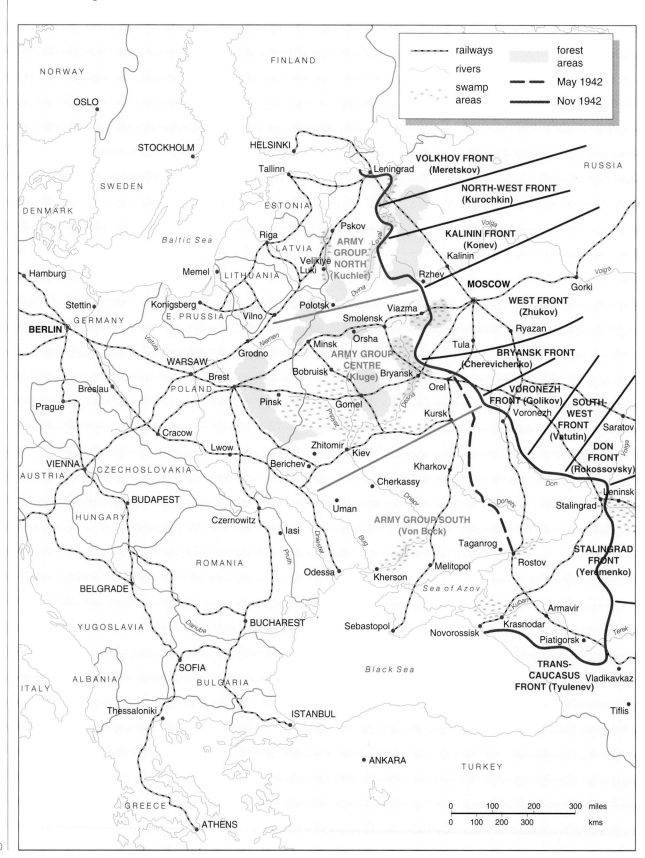

RIGHT *A 1942 Soviet I153 'White 50' of 71.IAP. (John Weal, from Aircraft of the Aces 15, Soviet Aces of World War II)*

FAR RIGHT *A 1942 SdKfz 251/1 Ausf.C of 24.Panzer-Division. (Bruce Culver, from New Vanguard 25, SdKfz 251 Half-Track)*

RIGHT *A Panzer III tries to pull a StuG III out of a snowdrift. German tanks were not designed for the temperatures they encountered in Russia, lubricants congealed and even the tracks froze to the snow. (Author's collection)*

BELOW *The one-horse sleigh represented one of the few reliable forms of transport for the German army in the winter of 1941–2. Winter clothing had been ordered for 60 of the 150-plus divisions in Russia, but as German supply arrangements collapsed little of it arrived at the front. (Author's collection)*

other vital strategic target, the Soviet rail network had been left alone too as all German aircraft were devoted to immediate tactical missions.

On the Moscow front from December to January the Red air force failed to pounce on the retreating German columns, even as they crowded along the few metalled roads that the engineers managed to keep open despite the snow falls.

The Red Army's advances trapped similar numbers of German troops behind the lines. Three important 'pockets' survived, largely by aerial resupply. At Demyansk, six German divisions under General von Seydlitz held out until late March. Later to play a key role at the battle of Stalingrad, Von Seydlitz was a veteran of Germany's previous war with Russia and had been involved in an earlier battle of encirclement at Brczeziny, near Lodz, in 1914. He led a break-out from Demyansk, an epic thirty-day battle of endurance that ended just as the spring thaw imposed a halt on operations. The ability of the Luftwaffe to sustain encircled German forces would be remembered the next winter, with disastrous consequences for the German 6th Army. What was overlooked was the sorry state of the survivors. The high command saw divisions rejoining, albeit without their heavy weapons. They could be replaced, but the mental and

physical consequences of living and fighting on the frozen steppe without nourishment, sanitation or medical facilities were harder to overcome.

Further south, an offensive south of Kharkov pushed a 70-mile salient into German lines and established a bridgehead on the west bank of the

Donets. An amphibious assault re-established a Russian presence on the Kerch peninsula, but the Russian 44th Army was unable to break out into the Crimea to relieve the siege of Sevastopol.

The spring thaw found the German army holding its positions some 180 miles west of Moscow, the sort of distance the Panzer spearheads had covered in less than a week in the summer of 1941. Small wonder then that Stalin concentrated his forces on the Moscow front in expectation of a renewed drive on the Soviet capital. On a map, the German threat looked more obvious yet, a salient centred on Rzhev pointed at Moscow like an arrowhead. Behind it lay the trapped Russian 33rd Army. To the north, Russian forces had driven the Germans back to Velikie Luki, the front line dipping south to within 60 miles of Smolensk. To the south, the Russian drive on Bryansk had been stopped well short of the city: Kursk, Belgorod and Kharkov all remained in German hands.

Casualties had been unprecedented. From the invasion to the end of November the Ostheer had suffered 743,000 casualties, of which 200,000 were dead. By comparison, German losses in the invasions of Belgium, Holland and France were 44,000 dead and 156,000 wounded. The fighting outside Moscow from December to January cost another 55,000 dead and 100,000 wounded. Panzer divisions were lucky to have 20 operational tanks by early 1942: three-quarters of the approximately 1,000 tanks assembled for Operation

LEFT *German 10cm field guns seen in early 1942. Note the absence of any precautions against air attack: the Soviet air force presented little threat at this stage of the war. Later in the war battery commanders would have to site their guns with anti-tank defence as a top priority. (Author's collection)*

CENTRE *As the snow melted the land became waterlogged, and dirt roads turned into sticky morasses, impassable for wheeled vehicles. Here a German staff car is dragged through the mud by a half-track. (R. Tomasi)*

BOTTOM *Romanian soldiers in the Kerch peninsula on the eastern tip of the Crimea, early 1942. The Romanian army suffered nearly 100,000 casualties in the battle for Odessa in late 1941, losing so many junior officers that its effectiveness in 1942 was significantly impaired. (R. Tomasi)*

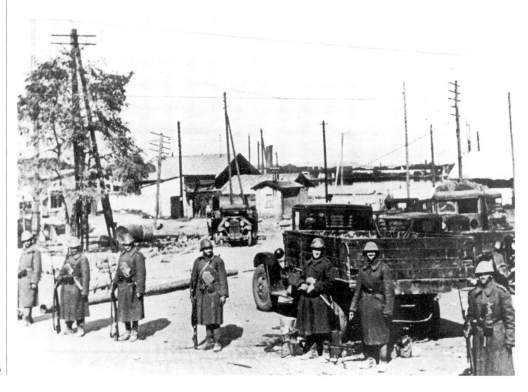

RIGHT *The capture of a partisan. Soviet soldiers trapped behind German lines formed the nucleus of a resistance movement. As the war went on, the German seizure of 2.8 million people as slave workers, more than half of them young women, drove many civilians into the partisan movement too. (Author's collection)*

CENTRE *The 800mm (31.5in.) calibre rail gun 'schwere Gustav', used by the Germans against Sevastopol, is the biggest gun ever to see action. It fired 48 shells weighing seven tons (armour-piercing) or ten tons (high explosive). Requiring 1,420 personnel to operate, schwere Gustav was a magnificent technical achievement but a dubious investment. It was dismantled after the siege and shipped back to Germany, never to see action again. (IWM)*

BELOW *Romanian cavalry in the Crimea, where they took part in the destruction of the Soviet bridgehead at Kerch in May 1942. With the peninsula once again under complete German control, there was no hope for the defenders of Sevastopol. (R. Tomasi)*

Typhoon were lost by 4 December. The Luftwaffe had lost 758 bombers, 568 fighters and 767 other aircraft destroyed: 473 bombers, 413 fighters and 475 other aircraft were damaged.

Soviet losses were astronomical. Every mechanised corps and 177 rifle divisions had been written off. About 1,000 vehicles remained from the pre-war tank fleet of some 22,000. The defence of Moscow and the counter-attack that followed had cost nearly a million casualties. Over three million Red Army soldiers[22] were taken prisoner in the headlong German advance of 1941. By February 1942, only about a quarter of a million remained alive.

BEHIND THE LINES

Many Red Army units caught behind the German lines in the initial invasion did not surrender. They melted into the forests and swamps, to re-emerge when the German forces had passed eastwards. As early as July 1941 German commanders were reporting attacks well behind the lines, launched by cut-off units of the Red Army and local volunteers. The Partisan war had begun.

Despite its previous association with guerrilla warfare, the Soviet regime discovered a severe shortage of experienced guerrilla commanders in 1941. Stalin had executed most of the Bolshevik 'Old Guard' and there had been no preparations for resistance activity in the late 1930s. All pre-war Soviet war plans assumed a conventional war in

LEFT *German soldiers in peaked caps and shorts near the mouth of the River Dnepr. The swamps and marshes here were among the few areas of cover where partisans could operate in the Ukraine. (Author's collection)*

BELOW LEFT *A 1942 SdKfz 251/3 Ausf.B, with a 2.8cm Panzerbuchs, of 3.Panzer-Division. Able to penetrate 56mm of armour at 350m, the sPzB41 was an improved anti-tank rifle, the bore tapering from 28mm at the breach to 20mm at the muzzle. It was originally built for airborne units, but some filtered through to the Panzer divisons. (Bruce Culver, from New Vanguard 25, SdKfz 251 Half-Track)*

BOTTOM *A 1941 LaGG-3 'White 6' of 178.IAP, 6 IAK PVO Moscow. The LaGG-3 was an improved version of the LaGG-1 introduced in early 1941. Armed with a 20mm cannon and two 12.7mm machine guns, it had adequate firepower but poor climb performance. Some 6,500 were built before production ceased in 1942. (John Weal, from Aircraft of the Aces 15, Soviet Aces of World War II)*

which the Red Army would take the offensive. Stalin's future successor, Nikita Khruschev (then Party boss in the Ukraine), issued the first call to arms in June 1941, with Stalin taking up the theme of guerrilla struggle in his radio address to the nation in July.

As the German advance swept deeper into the USSR, so NKVD and party officials attempted to organise guerrilla units in its wake. Initial attempts were not successful. In the open country of the Ukraine there was nowhere for the partisans to hide and the local population was welcoming the German tanks with flowers. Resistance efforts

foundered in the Crimea too, where the disaffected Tartar population helped the Germans hunt down the guerrillas. The NKVD continued its mass arrests in the Baltic republics but the Red Terror proved as counter-productive as later German policies. Local people anticipated the arrival of the Germans and began attacking Soviet installations.

By early 1942 the Partisan movement had yet to make a serious impact on the war. Although a central command system had been created in Moscow to co-ordinate the campaign behind the lines, there were probably no more than 30,000 guerrillas in the field.[23] However, a nucleus had been created. The remnants of Red Army units, in some areas reinforced by forces cut off after the failed counter-offensives in the spring combined with party activists and locals who had discovered the nature of Hitler's 'New Order' for themselves. The blind savagery with which the German army treated the conquered peoples of the USSR soon alienated many potential sympathisers. And news spread of the ghastly prisoner-of-war camps, where over two million soldiers had met their deaths over the winter.

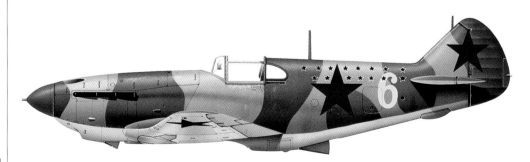

Behind the Russian lines men and women were struggling to survive too. In sub-zero temperatures, sometimes in near-total darkness, they unloaded machine tools from rail cars and reassembled whole factories in remote areas. The success with which Soviet industry was evacuated east in 1941 was justly celebrated by the USSR as a triumph as significant as any victory on the battlefield. Indeed, it would be the foundation of all subsequent victories. Iron, steel and engineering plants were shipped to the Urals, Siberia or Kazakhstan on some 1.5 million wagon loads.

Sixteen million people went with them, labouring with grim determination to get the machines turning again. The Yak fighter factory in Moscow was dismantled and shipped to Siberia where production resumed after just six days on site. In three months production exceeded the quotas achieved in Moscow.

The Herculean efforts of the Soviet industrial workforce enabled the Red Army to re-equip in time for the 1942 campaigns. Many German memoirs stress the overwhelming numerical superiority of Soviet forces, but this was more apparent than real in the second year of the Russo-German war. In 1942 it was Germany that enjoyed every industrial advantage, with the factories of most of Europe at her disposal. German steel production, for example, was four times that of the USSR.[24] Nevertheless, even in the second half of 1941 in the middle of the relocation programme, the USSR built more tanks than German factories delivered in the whole year. Soviet factories delivered 4,500 tanks, 3,000 aircraft and 14,000 artillery pieces to the Red Army by May 1942. Over that whole year, Soviet production figures would reach 24,000 tanks and self-propelled guns, 127,000 guns and mortars and 25,000 aircraft. Comparable German figures were 9,000 tanks, 12,000 guns and mortars and 15,000 aircraft. Note the yawning disparity in artillery manufacture. The story of the war behind the front line will be explored more fully in Chapter 6.

The growing gulf in Soviet and German industrial production would not begin to

transform the situation at the front until late 1942. Meanwhile, as the floods caused by the spring thaw began to subside, both sides prepared to take the offensive – and in the same area.

THE DRIVE SOUTH

The Soviet blow fell first. Marshal Timoshenko presided over an ambitious combined-arms offensive intended to recover Kharkov and advance on the Dnepropetrovsk-Sinelnikovo axis to recapture the main crossing points over the River Dnepr. The attack began on 12 May, Soviet forces

breaking through the thinly-manned German front to advance 15km. Although it quickly became apparent that the Germans were in much greater strength than had been assumed, the advance continued and the 3rd Guards Cavalry Corps was brought forward to exploit the breakthrough. The following events only served to highlight the difference between the inexperienced Soviet commanders and the veterans of the German 6th and 17th armies opposing them. The Soviet thrust was parried by the 6th Army, but not stopped. As Timoshenko's forces pressed steadily west, the 17th Army prepared and executed a sudden lunge at the Izyum bridgehead, smashing two Russian tank corps that turned back to defend it. By 22 May the Russian spearheads were encircled. The Soviet 6th, 9th and 57th Armies were cut off and destroyed. Total losses were 237,000 men. Timoshenko flew to Moscow, suspecting he might be shot, but although relieved of his command he was sent to command the North-Western Front in July.

Just as the Kharkov offensive turned into a major disaster, the Red Army lost its hard-won foothold on the Crimea. Its commanders dominated by the sinister Commissar Mekhlis, the Crimean Front had three lines of fortifications between it and the German 11th Army which was supposedly reducing Sevastopol. On 8 May Von Manstein's forces launched a surprise attack, breaking through each line in turn. In fine spring weather, the rejuvenated Luftwaffe annihilated the

RIGHT *German engineers blow up a gun turret on one of the Soviet forts protecting Sevastopol. The garrisons fought on after their big guns were silenced, leading to savage battles in the tunnels and casemates with flame-throwers, hand grenades and demolition charges. (US National Archives)*

BELOW *German engineers in the Crimea, July 1942, probably rehearsing for the assault on Sevastopol. Even with massive artillery and air support, German forces still lost over 75,000 men in the battle. (US National Archives)*

Soviet air regiments and bombed the rapidly shrinking bridgehead from dawn to dusk. Attempts by the Black Sea Fleet to extract survivors from the beaches were punished with air and artillery bombardments, and when resistance ceased on 19 May, the Crimean Front had lost 350 tanks, 3,500 guns and suffered 176,000 casualties. Mekhlis was demoted along with most of the senior officers who presided over the debacle.

With the Kerch bridgehead eliminated, the naval base of Sevastopol was hopelessly isolated.

The landward approaches were defended by giant concrete and steel fortifications, forts 'Stalin', 'Molotov', 'Siberia' and 'Maxim Gorky'. Their heavy guns duelled with German artillery until a combination of gargantuan siege guns and constant air attack silenced them. The German siege train included the 60cm (24in.) mortar 'Karl' and the 80cm (31in.) calibre railway gun 'Gustav'. The latter was the biggest gun ever built, originally intended to breach the Czech Sudetenland and French Maginot line defences. Its 7-tonne

armour-piercing shells destroyed a Soviet ammunition bunker under Severnaya Bay, passing through the water and 100ft of rock before detonating inside the magazine. Its HE rounds weighed over 10 tonnes and were used to pulverise one fort after another. Even then, it took teams of combat engineers with flame-throwers and grenades to storm the strong points, connected by underground tunnels. It was horribly reminiscent of the battle of Verdun in 1916, although Von Manstein took care to maximise the use of engineers, artillery and air power rather than squander his infantry.

The Luftwaffe flew some 23,000 sorties to deliver 20,529 tons of bombs on Sevastopol in three weeks. (By comparison, the Luftwaffe dropped 21,860 tons of bombs on the whole of the UK during the 1941 'Blitz'.) German artillery fired 562,944 rounds. The assault began on 7 June and by the end of the month it was clear that resistance could not be sustained. Destroyers could enter the port by night, but the remorseless German advance brought their guns in line with the harbour. Submarines continued to deliver ammunition and take off a lucky few of the wounded, but the bulk of the 106,000-strong garrison fought and died in the ruined forts, bunkers and the rubble of their city. The last centres of resistance were overwhelmed in early July and Von Manstein was promoted to Field Marshal. Of the approximately 30,000 civilians left in Sevastopol, two-thirds were deported or executed.

As the guns fell silent at Sevastopol, Hitler moved his headquarters to Vinnitsa in the Ukraine to oversee a new and enormously ambitious offensive. Although some of his senior commanders,

most notably Admiral Raeder, argued that Germany should remain on the defensive in Russia while attacking in the Mediterranean, Hitler's attention was focused almost exclusively on the East. That he would continue to concentrate on the Russian front, and site his HQ in East Prussia until the end of 1944, demonstrates its overriding importance to him. It also exposes the limits of his horizons. In what was now a world war involving four continents, Hitler remained obsessed with the Eastern front and would attempt to micro-manage the campaign there, while critical events in other theatres passed him by.

Hitler's target in 1942 was the Soviet oil industry. By seizing the oil fields of the Caucasus he would solve the oil shortage that bedevilled the German war machine, and deprive the USSR of its main source of fuel. The German army would strike past the junction of the Don and Donets, seizing Rostov on one flank and Stalingrad on the other. The Volga was a vital waterway for the

RIGHT *In one month, Sevastopol was hit by more bombs than fell on Britain in the whole of 1941. Here a German half-track noses through the rubble. (R. Tomasi)*

BELOW RIGHT *1941 PzKpfw III Ausf.H of 10.Panzer-Division, displaying its vehicle serial number '621'. The Ausf.H entered service in 1940 and carried the L/42 50mm gun. (David Smith)*

LOWER RIGHT *A 1942 PzKpfw III Ausf.J of 24.Panzer-Division. Entering service at the end of 1941, the Ausf.J had additional armour, bringing frontal protection up to 50mm. This was already inadequate compared to the T-34. (David Smith)*

BOTTOM RIGHT *A 1943 PzKpfw III Ausf.J belonging to 1.SS-Panzer-Division 'Leibstandarte Adolf Hitler'. It is seen towards the end of Manstein's counter-offensive at Kharkov in late February 1943. White camouflage has been painted over the standard grey finish. (David Smith)*

USSR, and the occupation of Stalingrad would block another logistic artery.

The shores of the Caspian sea lay 400 miles south-east of the front line. But to undertake this dramatic advance, the German army had less than half the forces available in 1941. A total of 68 divisions, including eight Panzer and seven motorised divisions, would take part in the offensive. Army Group Centre retained the balance of German armour, but its divisions were at very reduced strength. The SS motorised divisions Leibstandarte, Das Reich and Totenkopf were withdrawn to France during 1942 to refit as Panzer divisions, reappearing to dramatic effect in February 1943. The absence of an armoured reserve in late 1942 would prove critical. Across the whole front, 3.25 million German soldiers faced a Red Army calculated by German intelligence at 5 million strong.[25] Whereas the Soviet mobilisation had conjured up 488 divisions in 1941 and would create another 134 during 1942, the German army had no reserve other than its garrisons in western Europe. To bulk out the numbers, Hitler pressurised his allies into contributing nearly three-quarters of a million personnel. Romania supplied 24 divisions, Italy and Hungary despatched ten each.

The German allied forces varied in motivation, training and equipment. The Romanians had already contributed heavily, suffering some 98,000 casualties in the battle for Odessa in 1941. This expended the best of their peacetime-trained formations and a terribly high proportion of their

officers. The Italian expeditionary force of three divisions sent to Russia in 1941 had suffered badly in the winter, lacking cold weather clothing and equipment. But Mussolini expanded it to become the Italian 8th Army, with a total strength of 229,000 men and 1,100 guns in April 1942. An infantry corps and an Alpine corps (with its supply column of 20,000 mules) were added during the summer, the latter earmarked for the Caucasus mountains.

The Luftwaffe concentrated almost its entire strength on the eastern front for the summer campaign. Against a Soviet air arm that was reduced to about 5,000 aircraft and unable to seriously interrupt German aerial missions, the Luftwaffe had a total of over 4,000 aircraft of which about 3,000 were deployed to Russia.[26]

The original German plan called for Army Group B (formerly Army Group South) to advance into the bend of the Don River, then drive on Stalingrad as one half of the traditional pincer movement. Army Group A (a new

LEFT *A Soviet position near Sevastopol overrun by the Germans. Soviet losses during the siege were approximately 250,000: the garrison received constant drafts of replacements until Manstein launched his main assault. (R. Tomasi)*

BELOW *German gunners with a 7.5cm infantry gun, used for direct support as in 1917–18. They are near the mouth of the Don, in summer 1942: note the mosquito nets worn by several of the team. (R. Tomasi)*

RIGHT *A 1943 Tiger E, 8/sPzKp, of 2.SS-Pz.-Gren.-Div. 'Das Reich'. This Tiger company was formed in December 1942 and first went into action in February 1943. (David Smith)*

BELOW RIGHT *Italian and German officers east of the River Don, October 1942. In little over a month, the Italian forces in Russia would suffer terrible losses as the Soviets counter-attacked either side of Stalingrad. (R. Tomasi)*

formation including 1st Panzer Army, 17th German and 3rd Romanian armies) would form the other pincer, taking Rostov before linking up with Army Group A in another battle of encirclement on the approaches to Stalingrad. With the Red Army driven back to the Volga, hopefully with heavy losses, Army Group A would then swing south and east to occupy the Caucasus oil fields.

July saw rapid advances, but they brought in relatively few prisoners. This time it seemed the Red Army was just running away. Meanwhile, on the central front where Stalin had expected the blow to fall, Zhukov launched an offensive north of Orel, inflicting heavy casualties on 2nd Panzer Army. The impatient Führer ordered Army Group A to take Rostov and advance along the eastern coast of the Black Sea while Army Group B was to detach 1st and 4th Panzer armies. While this armoured force struck at Maikop, Grozny and Baku, the rest of Army Group B continued towards the Volga.

The 4th Panzer Army was soon returned to Army Group B, supporting the German 6th Army which reached the outer suburbs of Stalingrad on 23 August. The honour of breaking into the city fell to the 79th Panzer Grenadier regiment, which captured the northerly suburb of Spartanovka just before midnight. Hitler's army had reached the Volga.

Had 4th Panzer remained with 6th Army in July, it might well have been able to seize the city then, but by the beginning of September it was clear the Russians were determined to hold Stalingrad. Unlike in 1941 the German army no longer had enough armoured forces to bypass

the city on either side and cut it off. It was going to have to make a frontal attack.

At the same time, Russian resistance in the Caucasus slowed the advance of Army Group A. Hitler sent General Jodl to investigate Field Marshal List's lack of progress, only to have his own instructions quoted back at him. The stifling heat of the Ukrainian summer did not make for cool tempers. In an incandescent rage, Hitler sacked List and announced that he would command the Army Group personally. He was so furious with his generals that he refused to take his meals with them at Vinnitsa. As for the hapless Jodl, he was to be replaced by a rising star in the Nazi firmament – the hitherto undefeated commander of the 6th Army, General Friederich Paulus,[27] whose men were fighting their way into Stalingrad.

CHAPTER FIVE

VERDUN ON THE VOLGA: THE BATTLE OF STALINGRAD

Stunned, we stared at our situation maps on which menacing thick red lines of encirclement and arrows showed enemy attacks ... We had never imagined a catastrophe of such proportions to be possible.

Joachim Wieder, Ic German 8th Army Corps

The battle of Stalingrad cost more lives than any other battle of World War II. The Germans and their allies suffered 800,000 casualties, while Russian losses were just over 1.1 million. It was the turning point of the war. The Wehrmacht was defeated so catastrophically that not even Goebbels' propaganda machine could conceal the extent of the disaster. Most families in Germany lost a relative or friend at Stalingrad. The invasion of Russia had been sold to the German people as a defensive measure, as much as a campaign for 'living space'. According to the Nazi view, German soldiers were advancing into Russia to protect western European civilisation against Bolshevism. Military reality and Nazi myth converged in the wake of Stalingrad. The war of conquest was now a struggle for survival.

The enduring image of Stalingrad is that of the desolate, frozen city that became the tomb of the German 6th Army. Yet the pitiless fighting that consumed most of Paulus' command took place across the snow-covered steppes to the west. It was only after Panzergruppe Hoth's relief effort failed and the airstrips were overrun that the final battle for the city began. And a significant proportion of the casualties had occurred before the first snows fell, in house-to-house fighting that lasted from mid-September to mid-November. On the Stalingrad front, from July to November 1942, the Red Army suffered 323,000 killed or missing, 319,000 wounded and lost 1,426 tanks and over 12,000 guns. Heavy casualties were sustained by newly-mobilised Russian infantry divisions, led by inexperienced officers trying to halt the advance of some of the most battle-hardened professional soldiers in the world. The German 6th Army had been fighting for two years, and if some veterans were beginning to wonder if they would ever get any leave, the army had justified pride in its unbroken run of victories.

As noted in Chapter 4, for the first time the German army was unable to simply sweep past a city, leaving the defenders to surrender – its standard procedure in 1941. With the much depleted armoured force already fully committed, the army was compelled to fight its way into an urban area, defended with desperate courage by Russian soldiers with the Volga (and Stalin) at their backs. Reports of the army's low morale, the panicked evacuation of Rostov and stampede back to Stalingrad had perturbed Moscow. *Ni Shagu Nazad!* – not a step backward! – was the theme of Stalin's Order 227 read out to Red Army units on 28 July. Draconian disciplinary measures were enforced, with a reported 13,500 soldiers executed that summer and many more consigned to newly-created Strafbats (penal battalions). These were effectively suicide units, employed as human mine-detectors or to spearhead assaults:

LEFT *Soviet troops in the battle for Stalingrad. From left to right: anti-tank rifleman, Red Army; rifleman, Red Army; senior sergeant, Red Army Tank Forces. The anti-tank rifle remained in service with the Soviet forces until the end of World War II, despite its inability to do more than scratch the paint of most main battle tanks. (Ron Volstad, from Men-at-Arms 216,* The Red Army of the Great Patriotic War 1941–45*)*

STALINGRAD, NOVEMBER 1942

With German Panzer divisions scattered from the Moscow front to the Caucasus, the 6th Army was obliged to assault Stalingrad frontally, rather than envelop it in the traditional manner. By late 1942 the battle for the city had absorbed almost all the German units in the sector, the long flanks guarded by less well equipped and less committed allied armies. The Soviet plan had worked.

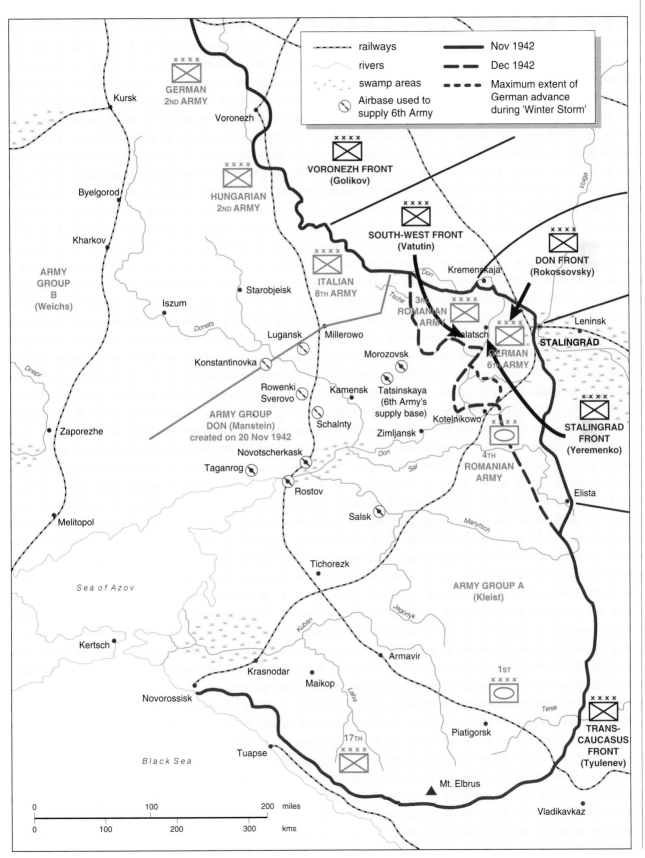

Legend:
- ·—·—· railways
- rivers
- swamp areas
- ⊘ Airbase used to supply 6th Army
- —— Nov 1942
- – – – Dec 1942
- ·· ·· ·· Maximum extent of German advance during 'Winter Storm'

Kursk

GERMAN 2ND ARMY

Voronezh

Byelgorod

VORONEZH FRONT (Golikov)

HUNGARIAN 2ND ARMY

Kharkov

SOUTH-WEST FRONT (Vatutin)

DON FRONT (Rokossovsky)

ARMY GROUP B (Weichs)

Volga

Kremenskaja

Leninsk

ITALIAN 8TH ARMY

Starobjeisk

Iszum

Donets

Tschir

Don

3RD ROMANIAN ARMY

GERMAN 6TH ARMY

STALINGRAD

Lugansk

Millerowo

Kalatsch

Dnepr

Konstantinovka

Morozovsk

Rowenki Sverovo

Kamensk

Tatsinskaja (6th Army's supply base)

STALINGRAD FRONT (Yeremenko)

Zaporezhe

ARMY GROUP DON (Manstein) created on 20 Nov 1942

Schalnty

Zimljansk

Kotelnikowo

Novotscherkask

Don

Sal

Taganrog

Rostov

4TH ROMANIAN ARMY

Melitopol

Salsk

Manytsch

Elista

Sea of Azov

Tichorezk

ARMY GROUP A (Kleist)

Jegorlyk

Kertsch

Kuban

Krasnodar

Maikop

Armavir

1ST

Novorossisk

Laba

Terek

Piatigorsk

TRANS-CAUCASUS FRONT (Tyulenev)

Tuapse

17TH

Black Sea

Mt. Elbrus

Vladikavkaz

| 0 | | 100 | | 200 | miles |
| 0 | 100 | 200 | 300 | | kms |

spectacular acts of bravery were required to win transfer back to a regular unit.

Reaching the Don on 23 July, the German army cut the last rail line between Moscow and Stalingrad, condemning Russian reinforcements to long road marches or rail journeys via central Asia. However, the whole German offensive was being conducted from a single low capacity railway, so both sides were fighting at the end of a tenuous supply line. In October, when the 6th Army was locked in bitter street fighting in the city, most of its horse transport was withdrawn. There seemed no sense wasting valuable train capacity on forage for draught animals for an army that was no longer moving. Still, Paulus was confident, giving his blessing to a commemorative patch that his men would wear after the victory: the German eagle presided over a picture of the gigantic grain silo – scene of intense fighting in September – with the legend 'STALINGRAD' emblazoned across the top.

Formerly the city of Tsaritsyn, Stalingrad had received the name of the Soviet dictator to commemorate the Bolshevik victory there during the civil war, a victory ascribed to the genius of Iosif Vissionarevitch. The name had a magnetic effect, drawing Hitler to insist on the capture of a city he did not need, and Stalin to sacrifice hundreds of thousands of men to defend it. Hitler's original view had been simply to stop Russian river traffic and not to get involved in a fight for the city. As he confessed to his old Nazi cronies at Munich's Löwenbräukeller on 8 November, 'I don't want a second Verdun'.

The city hugged the west bank of the river for nearly 15 miles, but was centred on three large manufacturing complexes; the Red October steel works, the Barrikady ordnance factory and the Stalingrad tractor factory. All three became centres of resistance. To attack the tractor factory in mid-October required the combined efforts of four German divisions with extra engineer battalions,

ABOVE *The Slovakian Mechanised Division was mainly equipped with ex-Czech tanks like this Panzer 38(t). Part of Panzergruppe Kleist, it advanced across the Kuban steppe in late 1942: it narrowly escaped encirclement in the retreat from the Caucasus that followed the defeat at Stalingrad. (R. Tomasi)*

LEFT *German walking-wounded stop for a Russian shoe-shine as they head back for treatment. As the battle for Stalingrad intensified, many German infantry companies were reduced to 30 or 40 men. (R. Tomasi)*

equipped for bunker fighting with flame-throwers and explosive charges, assaulting on a frontage of less than 5,000 yards. The city centre was defended by the Russian 62nd Army with some 54,000 men, 900 guns and mortars and some 110 tanks.[28] The German 6th Army had 25 divisions, with over 100,000 men committed to the battle for the city, supported by some 2,000 guns, 500 tanks and VIII Fliegerkorps, the latter providing over 1,000 sorties a day.

The battle for the city began in earnest on 13 September. The German 295th, 71st and 94th infantry divisions and 29th Motorised Division, supported by 14th and 24th Panzer divisions, launched an all-out attack which overran the low hill (height 102m) where the Soviet 62nd Army's HQ had been located. The railway station was taken and the 71st Division advanced far enough to bring the Volga landing stage under fire. With German outposts on the Volga, it seemed as if General Lopatin, commander of the Russian 62nd Army, was right – the city was going to fall. But Lopatin had been sacked 48 hours earlier. In his role as political trouble-shooter, Nikita Khruschev took charge and appointed Vasily Ivanovich Chuikov to replace him.

Once a teenage Bolshevik officer in the civil war, Chuikov was the archetypal Red Army general. Son of a peasant farmer, he obeyed Stalin's orders without question. British officers encountered him after the war as commander of Soviet forces in Berlin. His drinking binges were the stuff of legend, and woe betide the junior officer who crossed him the morning after. Chuikov survived

the purges to command a rifle corps by 1938 and the 9th Army in 1940. A dismal performance in Finland saw him consigned to China as the Soviet military attaché, something that Soviet histories of World War II would gloss over for the next fifty years because Chuikov redeemed himself at Stalingrad. His army (redesignated 8th Guards in April 1943) subsequently fought all the way to Berlin, and it was his headquarters that accepted the German surrender on 2 May 1945. With Khruschev's accession, Chuikov became a Marshal in 1955 and did not retire until 1971. He was buried with great ceremony at Volgograd (Stalingrad) in 1982. The 8th Guards Army, due to be disbanded after the Soviet withdrawal from Eastern Europe, was reprieved by President Yeltsin. The defenders of Stalingrad have not been forgotten.

The German assault brought the front line to within half a mile of Chuikov's new headquarters in a bunker by the Tsaritsa. He committed his last reserve of 19 T-34s, ordering the commander to hold or be shot (he was killed in action) and summoning the 13th Guards Division, then assembling on the east bank of the Volga. The Guards ran a gauntlet of machine gun and artillery fire to establish a bridgehead from which they made a succession of sharp counter-attacks. Committed piecemeal, the target of repeated Luftwaffe air strikes, the Guards Division suffered terribly, but the German advance stopped.

In ferocious house-to-house fighting, most of the city's wooden buildings were destroyed, leaving the soldiers to fight over rubble, through

LEFT *A Soviet anti-aircraft truck with its dead crew. The four Maxim guns have been removed. Luftwaffe pilots reported that heavy calibre Soviet flak was relatively ineffective, but at low altitudes they faced a hail of small arms fire. (Novosti)*

BELOW LEFT *Soviet aircraft from the defence of Stalingrad. A Yak-1 'Yellow 44' of 296.IAP. B Yak-7B 'White 31' of 434.IAP. C P-400 Airacobra BX728, 19.Gv.IAP. D P-40K Warhawk of 436.IAP, Northern Fleet Air Force. Soviet fighters were able to inflict heavy losses on the lumbering German transports flying to Stalingrad because there were very few German fighters available for escort duties. (John Weal, from Aircraft of the Aces 15, Soviet Aces of World War II)*

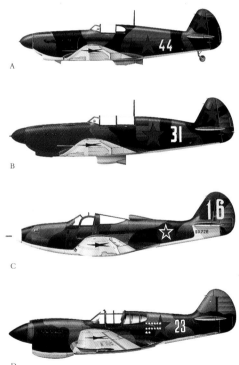

were appalling. The 13th Guards Division arrived nearly 10,000 strong, but only a few hundred men were still in action by the time 2,000 replacements arrived a month later.

Chuikov's army bled to death, fighting on in an ever-shrinking bridgehead. Chuikov was forced to relocate his headquarters again, this time in open trenches half-a-mile north of the Red October landing-stage. Engineers dug bunkers unaware nearby oil storage tanks were still full, their ignition during an air raid nearly immolated the entire staff. Drafts of replacements were fed in, just enough to keep the units operational, although divisions were often reduced to little more than battalions. The 92nd Rifle Brigade (naval infantry from the Baltic and Northern Fleets) arrived on 17 September with the 137th Tank Brigade. Major counter-attacks just north of the city failed to relieve the pressure, the German 6th Army smashing each one in turn, barely pausing in its effort to storm the city.

THE TRAP IS SET

Paulus flew to Vinnitsa for a meeting with Hitler on the eve of the September offensive. He was confident then, and remained convinced he could take the city almost to the moment the great Soviet counter-attack began in November. The very same day, Zhukov and Rokossovsky presented their plan for a full-scale counter-offensive, aimed at encircling the German 6th Army. The fate of Paulus' army was being plotted before it had even begun its assault on Stalingrad. Zhukov and

cellars and among the giant industrial complexes that resisted the heaviest bombardment. Because each assault left the attackers so disorganised, short of men and ammunition, counter-attacks often succeeded and the same objective could change hands repeatedly. The railway station captured by the Germans on the morning of 14 September was retaken within an hour, but stormed again by the Germans the same morning, only to be recaptured by the Russians in the afternoon. Casualties

RIGHT *A 1943 Soviet KV-1S of the 121st Tank Brigade as seen on the Stalingrad front in December 1942. This unit was equipped with tanks paid for by the villagers around the giant Tankograd factory complex at Chelyabinsk. (Steven Zaloga)*

BELOW *A StuG III provides direct support for German infantry in their final attempt to take Stalingrad, late November 1942. Within days the winter weather set in and the Soviets counter-attacked outside the city. (US Army Signal Corps)*

Rokossovsky foresaw how the battle for the city would soak up battalions, regiments, whole divisions – and that the main body of the 6th Army would be sucked into the maelstrom, leaving its long flanks guarded by second-rate units.

As the German offensive ran its course in the summer of 1942, the Red Army had continued to grow. The staggering casualties of 1941 had been almost completely replaced by the spring of 1942. The replacement divisions were untrained men with unfamiliar weapons led by novice officers. Their 'on-the-job' training in battle cost them dearly, but learn they did, buying time for another 40 divisions mobilised in early 1942 to train harder and longer before going to the front. Three more tank corps were added to the Soviet order of battle between May and November 1942. Rather than feed the new formations into battle as they assembled, the Red Army created a powerful reserve. With this new force, Zhukov and Rokossovsky planned not just to cut off the Germans in Stalingrad, but to push all the way to the Black Sea coast and amputate Army Group A. A third, and potentially the most decisive blow, would fall simultaneously on Army Group Centre, thus smashing the entire Ostheer.

Army Group A had driven rapidly into the Caucasus, conducting a 1941-style Blitzkrieg across the Kuban during August. The Soviet naval base at Novorossisk was overrun, and Maikop fell, although not before the oil installations were blown up by the Russians. The advance continued across the baking steppe, temperatures topping 50°C. Ahead lay the mountains of the Caucasus,

LEFT *German troops with either very tame prisoners or, more likely, Hilfswillige. By mid-1942 most divisions of the Ostheer had Russians or Ukrainians working as service troops. They did not appear on the ration strength, so their fate at Stalingrad was predictably grim. (R. Tomasi)*

BELOW *Like most Russian cities, Stalingrad had a high proportion of single-storey wooden houses: most burned down during the German attack. (Author's collection)*

visible for miles as a line of cloud on the horizon. On 21 August a team from the German 1st Mountain Division planted the German flag on Mount Elbrus, at 18,481ft (5,633m) the highest mountain in the Caucasus. Fighting their way over the mountain passes, the men of 49th Mountain Corps entered the sub-tropical forest surrounding Sukhumi.

Some 200 miles east, the Russian forces protecting the oil fields around Grozny had been driven back to their last line of defence, the River Terek. At the end of August Panzergruppe Kleist seized the first of several bridgeheads over the river. Meanwhile, elements of the 16th Motorised Division had driven to the outskirts of Astrakhan on the Caspian sea. The strategic objectives of Baku and Tiflis were tantalisingly close, but Army Group A was 600 miles south of Stalingrad and had out-run its supply lines. Bringing forward the replacements, ammunition and equipment for the last push took most of October. In a final attempt to break through, Kleist renewed the assault on 1 November, the 13th Panzer Division penetrating to within a few miles of Ordzhonikidze before a Soviet counter-attack forced it to withdraw or be encircled.

The German offensive at Stalingrad continued, long after General Weichs, commander of Army Group B begged Hitler to call it off. In public speeches Hitler committed himself to taking Stalingrad. German soldiers had reached the Volga and no power on earth could shift them

RIGHT *A 6th Army StuG in Stalingrad on the eve of the great German assault in mid-October 1942. Most of the city was captured, leaving the Soviets clinging to a few small bridgeheads with their backs to the Volga. (Bundesarchiv)*

from it. In a situation briefing at his headquarters on 2 October, he told the High Command that 'world opinion and the morale of our allies' demanded the capture of Stalingrad. Paulus regrouped his forces and stock-piled ammunition, then struck on 14 October, aiming at the Tractor and Barrikady factories. For two weeks the fighting raged day and night, German combat engineer teams spearheading each assault with flame throwers and explosive charges. Tanks surrounded by infantry protection teams fired into Soviet strong points at point blank range, and Stukas appeared over Stalingrad every morning, bombing with great precision. By November only ten per cent of the city remained in Russian hands, the ruins of the Tractor factory were finally captured and Chuikov's army was split in two. The 6th Army gathered itself for a final effort before winter, attacking the Red October steel works with nine divisions on 11–12 November. By this stage in the battle, front-line rifle companies were reduced to 30 or 40 men. The 6th Army had only 180 operational tanks.[29] The same night, German intelligence repeated its warnings about Russian armies massing along the 300km front held by Romanian, Italian and Hungarian forces. These allied formations were far less well equipped than German units, for instance, the Romanian divisional anti-tank units had horse-drawn 37mm guns, weapons that had proved unable to stop T-34s over a year previously. Their field guns were a mixture of old Austrian and French weapons for which there were no ammunition stocks available in the German logistic system. The Romanian infantry divisions were trying to hold frontages of over 20km each.

Halder's diaries chronicle the Führer's retreat into fantasy that autumn, an escalating practise of denial that would culminate in his withdrawal to the Berlin bunker in 1945, still transmitting orders to non-existent armies to march to his rescue. News that Russian tank production now exceeded 1,200 vehicles a month produced a spectacular tirade – but no change in policy.[30] Halder was himself sacked in October, his successor General Kurt Zeitzler also urging a withdrawal from Stalingrad, also to no avail. However, the idea that Hitler ignored clear warnings of the forthcoming Soviet offensive[31] should be treated with caution. In fact OKH had little indication of what was to come. Gehlen's team had identified a threat to the 6th Army's northern flank and moved the 48th Panzer Corps to cover it. (Consisting of 22nd Panzer Division – 45 operational tanks – and the 1st Romanian Tank Division – 40 Czech R–2 tanks – this was all that was available.) The Germans never realised the attack would be on such a scale, and there was no hint that the Russians would attack to the south of Stalingrad too.

Three Soviet Fronts (South-West, Don and Stalingrad) with a combined strength of 1.1

million men, 894 tanks and 12,000 guns began the great winter offensive on 19 November. At Stalingrad itself, the dawn was barely perceptible, the gaunt silhouettes of the ruined tower blocks hidden in the fog. The gloom never lifted, and in the afternoon came the first heavy snowstorm. The city and the surrounding steppe were about to be engulfed in the terrible Arctic winter. The initial bombardment of the thinly-stretched German front was supplemented by the thunderous roar of a hundred multiple-rocket launcher batteries, used en masse for the first time. About 1,200 Soviet aircraft had been deployed to support the Fronts. The sudden concentration of Russian fighters and the onset of severe weather ended the Luftwaffe's domination of the Stalingrad area.

The Russians swept through the Romanian and Italian armies, Luftwaffe field divisions, security units and other formations dotted along the south bank of the Don. The encirclement was completed on 23 November, when the two Russian spearheads met at Kalatsch. The Russians did not know it, but they had trapped about 300,000 German and allied troops in the Stalingrad pocket. The entire 6th Army was there, the bulk of 4th Panzer Army; 20 divisions belonging to four army corps and a Panzer corps There were 13 infantry divisions, three Panzer

divisions, three motorised divisions, a Luftwaffe flak division, field artillery regiments including two Sturmgëschutz battalions, a dozen combat engineer battalions, a Croat regiment attached to a Jäger division, construction units, medical services, elements of the Reichs labour service, the 20th Romanian Infantry and 1st Cavalry Division as well as survivors of the Romanian forces who had escaped eastwards into the pocket. Thousands of Russian Hilfswillige – civilian service personnel who had volunteered or been press-ganged into most German divisions by 1942 – were also present, but as they never appeared on official ration strengths, their dreadful fate is practically unrecorded.

The encirclement caught the 6th Army without its winter clothing; this was at the army's supply depots of Tatsinskaya and Morozovsk, outside the perimeter. Once again, German soldiers would have to endure sub-zero temperatures, wearing summer uniforms padded with newspaper and straw. And the army only had food and fuel for a week. Paulus signalled Army Group Don on 22 November: 'Fuel will soon be exhausted. Tanks and heavy weapons then immovable. Ammunition situation strained. Food provisions sufficient for six days. Army intends to hold remaining area from Stalingrad to Don.

ABOVE *An MG34 machine gun team of the 6th Army outside Stalingrad. This was the standard machine gun of the infantry companies and provided most of their firepower. (IWM)*

RIGHT *A 1942 LTvz35 of the Romanian 1st Tank Regiment, which served at Stalingrad. The Romanian 1st Tank Division was practically annihilated at Stalingrad. In early 1943 Germany re-equipped the formation with 50 PzKpfw 38(t)s. (Terry Hadler, from New Vanguard 26, German Light Panzers 1932–42)*

Supposition is that closure of the South-West Front succeeds and adequate provisions will be flown in.'

Damaged equipment was blown up in expectation of an immediate order to break out. The Corps commanders were adamant that the army should fight its way back to German lines. Hube (14th Panzer Corps), Heitz (8th Corps) Jänicke (4th Corps) and Strecker (11th Corps) argued bitterly with Paulus and his chief-of-staff who insisted that they obey Hitler and dig in. Although a defensive front was quickly established facing west, there were no real defensive positions on the open steppe. The troops entrenched themselves as well as they could in the frozen earth and snow, but the expression '*Festung Stalingrad*' that appeared on one of the earliest OKH orders gave 6th Army staff officers their first clue that the High Command had no idea of local conditions. From the very beginning of the Stalingrad disaster, the 6th Army staff officers suspected the worst while the front-line troops remained confident. Hitler had ordered them to hold on. Soon they were told that 'Manstein will get you out'.

The Demyansk pocket had held out the previous winter because the Luftwaffe had been able to supply the men inside – albeit at great cost in aircraft (265 Ju-52s).[32] Now Reichmarshall Göring made his fateful promise to supply Stalingrad. Without reference to his staff officers, in complete ignorance of the 6th Army's requirements and the Luftwaffe's transport capabilities, Göring told Hitler he could supply Paulus' men by air. The Reichsmarschall's reputation had been

in tatters since May; RAF Bomber Command's 1,000 bomber raid on Cologne, and subsequent heavy raids made mockery of his bombastic pronouncements that Germany would never be bombed. Göring knew Hitler wanted to hold the city: by promising the Luftwaffe could make it possible, he sought to redeem his position within the Nazi hierarchy.

The major airfields from which the operation was to be mounted (Tatsinskaya and Morozovskaya-west) were just over 100 miles from the pocket. Eleven gruppe of Ju-52s and Ju-86s (600 aircraft) operated from Tatsinskaya and 400 from Morozovskaya-west, soon supplemented by Heinkel He-111s. A *gruppe* of Fw 200s and Ju-290s flew from Stalino while gigantic Messerschmitt Me-323s and Gotha 242s made the journey from Makeyevka in the Ukraine. Fighter cover was essential and a handful of Messerschmitt Bf-109s from the Udet wing flew into the pocket to operate from Pitomnik, the best airstrip inside the pocket.

Air crew were pulled off training to fly transports to Stalingrad. Nazi party leaders generously donated the services of their personal aircraft and their hitherto pampered crews. Russian fighters (especially the new La-5), concentrations of anti-aircraft weapons deployed along their predictable routes, and the truly savage winter weather combined to slaughter the transport squadrons. About a thousand aircrew died. Aircraft losses were 266 Ju-52s, 42 Ju-86s, 165 He-111s, 9 Fw 200s, five He-177s and one Ju-290. And it was followed by a similar massacre of German

of 140 Ju-52s operational, 41 out of 140 He-111s and just one of the 20 temperamental Fw 200s was air worthy.

Although Pitomnik was the best airstrip inside the pocket, it was not equipped for night operations and daytime flights soon became prohibitively dangerous. Two weeks after the encirclement, under the personal direction of the commander of the Red Army's Air Chief, General Novikov, the fighters were shooting down nearly half the lumbering transports heading for Stalingrad. From mid-December flying was largely restricted to nights or cloudy days, but the weather often closed in on the airstrips, preventing any flying at all. On the other hand, the airlift was practically suspended for the first week of January when clear skies left the transports nowhere to hide. Even daytime landings were hazardous and crews began to drop supplies by parachute instead. Towards the end, the 6th Army was so short of petrol it could not gather up or move heavy containers, so supplies piled up around Pitomnik while men starved to death only a few miles away.

The 6th Army's artillery and armoured vehicles were practically immobilised by the lack of fuel, although some reserves were hoarded for a break-out. The 6th Army had no stockpiles of food and hunger turned to starvation as the weeks slipped by. The bread ration was 200g (8oz) a day for men in the front line, and half that for the rear echelon. The steady slaughter of the remaining

LEFT *Junkers Ju-52s at a German depot on the Black Sea, autumn 1942. Some 500km further east, German troops were approaching Astrakhan on the shores of the Caspian.* (R. Tomasi)

BELOW *A German anti-tank gun ready for use against a Soviet strongpoint in Stalingrad.* (R. Tomasi)

transport aircraft over Tunisia – 'Tunisgrad' as it was dubbed. When Field Marshal Milch was belatedly sent to rescue the situation in mid-January 1943, he discovered a situation of utter chaos at the airfields supplying Stalingrad. Ground crew had no proper quarters and were trying to work on aircraft parked in the open in temperatures of -30°C. Ignorance of cold-start procedures[33] and other problems left only 15 out

transport animals provided another 200g of horse-flesh, 30g of cheese and 30g of butter. This was utterly inadequate for men fighting in extreme cold.

The sacrifice of the Luftwaffe's transport groups brought the 6th Army a daily delivery of about 100 tons of supplies over the duration of the siege, although over the first weeks it was only 60 tons or so – only enough for a single division. The 6th Army had requested a minimum of 500 tons per day - which was itself a gross underestimation as Paulus, a career staff officer,[34] knew very well when he made it. The figure actually refers to the supply requirements of Seydlitz's 51st Corps, which he had calculated at 400 tons of ammunition alone (per division per day); a figure which would double in case of heavy combat. Even on half-rations and with light combat, 51st Corps needed 598 tons (295 Ju-52 loads) per day or 990 tons (495 Ju-52 flights) in case of heavy fighting.

The barest minimum quantity of supplies required by Paulus' troops was about 1,500 tons per day. So the idea that the Luftwaffe could sustain the beleaguered army was not just unlikely, it was absolutely impossible. Several senior officers protested, including Fiebig (8th Air Corps) and Pickert (9th Flak Division). Richtofen (Luftflotte IV) wrote in his diary: 'The 6th Army believes it will be supplied by the air fleet … Every effort is being made to convince the army that it cannot be done'. Other Luftwaffe officers assumed that all they were trying to do was deliver as many supplies as possible before the 6th Army broke out. Yet the German high command persisted in maintaining the myth that aerial supply could keep the 6th Army operational. Perhaps, like Hitler they pinned their faith on the conqueror of Sevastopol, the apostle of Blitzkrieg who had planned the Ardennes breakthrough in 1940, Germany's newest Field Marshal, Erich von Manstein.

OPERATION WINTER STORM

Manstein assumed command of Army Group Don on 26 November, signalling Paulus the same day with a promise to do everything to get him and his men out. Only 48 hours earlier he had sent a signal to OKH, agreeing with Von Weichs' judgement that 6th Army must break out at once because it would run out of fuel by the time a relief force could be assembled.

It took two weeks to stabilise the front and muster enough forces to make a serious attempt. Generaloberst Hoth, commander of 4th Panzer Army, received the 23rd Panzer Division (hurried back from the Caucasus) and the 6th Panzer Division transferred by rail from France, followed by 17th Panzer Division detached from Army

FAILURE OF THE RELIEF EFFORT, DECEMBER 1942

The German attempt to relieve the 6th Army was a case of too little and too late. The controversy continues to this day as to whether Paulus should have ordered his men to break out, or whether

Manstein should have defied Hitler and ordered it himself. In the event, Zhukov's renewed attacks to the north drew off a major part of the relief column and the 6th Army was left to its hideous fate.

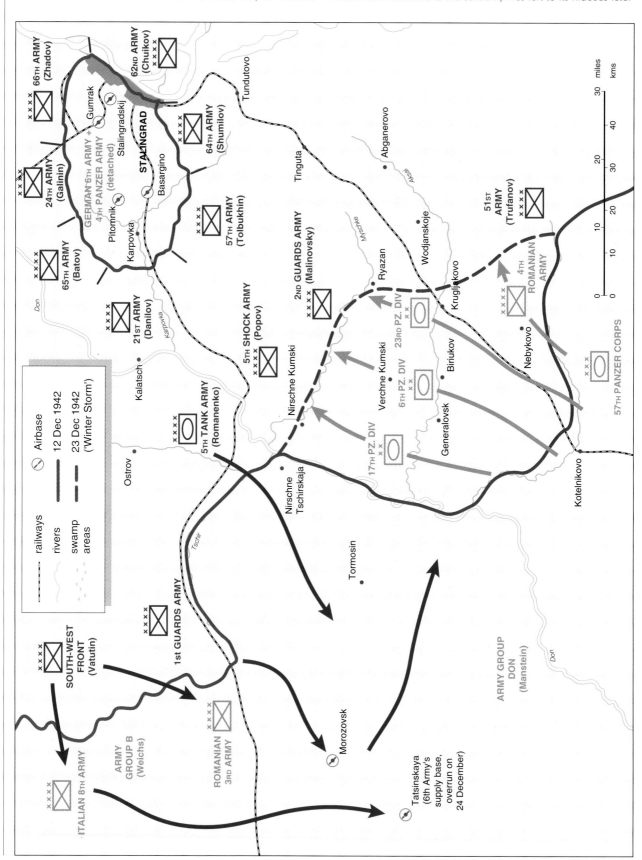

RIGHT *A Panzer IV(kz)
of 14th Panzer Division,
one of the three Panzer
divisions to be surrounded
at Stalingrad. This
picture was taken at the
end of October: by
mid-November only
41 tanks remained
operational. (Author's
collection)*

Group Centre. It was a perilously small force for such an undertaking, but Army Group Centre was itself the target of a major Soviet offensive, planned and led by Zhukov. In Operation Mars the Kalinin and Western Fronts attacked the salient at Rzhev, intending to encircle the German 9th Army and drive on Smolensk. This prevented Army Group Centre from assisting the southern German armies, and was presented as a diversionary operation by post-war Soviet accounts but its objectives were actually more ambitious than the Stalingrad encirclement. Zhukov intended the complete destruction of Army Group Centre, but although Velikie Luki was encircled and overrun, the offensive was defeated with heavy losses – largely because Army Group Centre had enough armoured forces to fight a mobile battle.[35]

No reinforcements were forthcoming from the west either, as on 8 November an Anglo-American army landed in North Africa (Operation Torch). German forces in the occupation zone of France were immediately ordered to take control of Vichy France and seize the French battlefleet at Toulon. Only after the danger of an amphibious invasion of southern France had passed were the armoured formations released to the eastern front. Of course, Hitler and OKW had no idea that the British would succeed in postponing the invasion of France into 1943 and finally to 1944, despite the US Army's wish to engage the Germans as soon as possible and America's mistrust of Britain's Mediterranean strategy. From the German perspective, the attack on North Africa appeared to be a prelude to an attack on Southern France.

Hoth began the rescue mission on 12 December. Two operations were planned: Winter Storm would punch through the Soviet encirclement to link the defenders of Stalingrad with the rest of the German army; then in Operation Thunderclap the 6th Army would escape westwards along the corridor carved by Hoth's Panzers. It was the latter which posed the greatest difficulty. Much of the 6th Army's horse transport had been withdrawn in October and there was too little fuel inside the pocket for the army's trucks (let alone tanks) to take part in a full-scale break-out. Fuel would have to be flown in, yet aerial deliveries were not even sufficient to maintain stocks at their existing levels. Manstein knew this within days of taking charge, and it makes nonsense of his suggestion in *Lost Victories* that Paulus should have ordered 'Thunderclap' without Hitler's permission. The 6th Army was stuck. Every day it held out saw its meagre supplies depleted further, steadily diminishing its chances of escape. An immediate flight to the west the moment the Soviet pincers met at Kalatsch might have saved the 6th Army, but Hitler would probably have sacked any officer ordering the break-out before the operation could have been accomplished.[36] On the other hand, General Jänicke and others believe the Führer would have retrospectively endorsed a decision to escape, as he did on later occasions.

The 6th Panzer Division began the relief attempt with 160 tanks, but 23rd Panzer had only 40 operational tanks on 18 November. The 17th Panzer Division had 60. Despite facing substantially larger Soviet forces, Hoth's 57th Panzer Corps fought its way forward about 30 miles in 12 days of intensive fighting. On the morning of 17 December, the 23rd Panzer Division captured two crossings over the River Aksay, bringing it within 45 miles of the 6th Army's perimeter. Then came the crushing news. A new Soviet offensive had opened (Operation Little Saturn) north-west of Stalingrad. The Soviet South-West Front attacked the Italian 8th Army and Romanian 3rd Army along the River Tschir, destroying them utterly. With the front broken open, powerful armoured formations thundered towards the vital airfields/supply depots at Tatsinskaya and Morozovsk. Major-general Badanov consciously drove his 24th Tank Corps far ahead of its supply columns, expending his command in order to seize Tatsinskaya, which his tanks overran on 24 December. Hitler's attempt to micro-manage the battle from his headquarters in East Prussia contributed to the ensuing disaster. He forbade General Fiebig to evacuate the airfield as requested on 23 December, permission only being granted as shells fell on the runway. Although 108 out of 180 Ju-52s escaped, struggling to get airborne with visibility down to 2,000ft, all the ground equipment was lost. Badanov's exhausted troops were driven off a few days later by a German counter-attack, but they destroyed the depot completely.[37]

Manstein was obliged to detach 6th Panzer to deal with the new threat, leaving Hoth to battle on alone. Grinding through the Soviet lines had reduced the Panzergruppe to just 35 tanks. The sound of the fighting could be heard from within the pocket. The 6th Army prepared its three strongest divisions to attack at Karpovka as soon as Hoth's troops were within 30km – there was not enough fuel for a longer advance. Starting with the Volga front, the encircled army planned to retreat south-west, units leapfrogging back with the army's remaining 100 armoured vehicles providing flank protection. Behind Hoth's battered spearhead the Germans assembled a supply column (2,300 tons capacity) to give 6th Army the ammunition and fuel it needed. Inside the pocket another column stood ready to take out thousands of wounded and sick, then return carrying 4,000 tons of supplies.

On clear nights, Hoth's soldiers could see flares on the distant horizon, rockets arcing high above the Stalingrad perimeter. But the relief effort was faltering. On 19 December, with the Soviet breakthrough along the Tschir menacing the airfields, Manstein ordered Paulus to prepare to launch not just Winter Storm but Thunderclap as well. 'Development of the situation may compel us to expand the mission' began the enigmatic last

LEFT German artillery in action in Stalingrad. In October many of the 6th Army's horses were withdrawn: they consumed too much fodder for the over-stretched supply system to deliver. (Author's collection)

RIGHT *Soldiers of the 6th Army in late autumn 1942. Their winter equipment was in depots over a hundred miles to the west, and they were still waiting for it when the Soviet attack encircled them. (Author's collection)*

BELOW *An Italian soldier stumbles in action on the flanks of the 6th Army, October 1942. The fighting in Stalingrad sucked in the bulk of German troops, leaving the long flanks guarded by much more lightly-equipped Allied formations. (R. Tomasi)*

section of his signal. The 'fortress area' (even he slipped into OKH wishful thinking) was to be evacuated sector by sector.

The order was not given. Conscious that his army had so little fuel left, it would soon be compelled to abandon its vehicles and guns. Neither Manstein nor Paulus would take responsibility for the break-out, an operation that would have seen the remains of the 6th Army try to fight its way across 50km of open steppe with nothing but rifles and shovels, abandoning their sick and wounded comrades to the enemy. Yet there can be no doubt that this superhuman task would have been made with exceptional determination, and as several of Paulus' officers said at the time, better to escape with six divisions than lose all 20. The British correspondent Alexander Werth was in Russia at the time, and visited Stalingrad immediately after the battle. He observed:

'judging from the Germans I saw in Stalingrad over six weeks later, they must still have been in reasonably good condition around 20 December;

they had by then been encircled for less than a month, and were not yet anywhere near real starvation. They also said they were "full of fight" at the thought of Von Manstein about to break through to Stalingrad. Even in January, those still in reasonably good condition fought with the greatest stubbornness during the Russian liquidation of the Cauldron.'[38]

The two commanders conferred by teleprinter on 19 December, the necessarily stilted exchange creating enough ambiguities to fuel post-war arguments about who was to blame for the ensuing disaster.[39]

The agonising at German headquarters was ended by General Rodion Yakovlevich Malinovksy and the Soviet 2nd Guards Army on Christmas Eve. Although Stalin berated his commanders for not immediately liquidating the pocket, the Red generals won the argument. The Soviet reserve was not flung against the city, but attacked the rest of Army Group Don. Tatsinskaya airfield was retaken from the survivors of the Soviet 24th Tank Corps, but recaptured by the Russians shortly afterwards. By 31 December, Hoth's relief force had been driven back beyond its start line and the German defensive front along the Don had collapsed. The Russian offensive had blown a gap over 200 miles wide, and the entire German Army Group in the Caucasus was in danger of being cut off.

The 6th Army was doomed. Several officers shot themselves. An understandable, but unedi-

fying scramble took place among the Nazi leadership to extract friends and relatives from Stalingrad before it was too late. Albert Speer tried and failed to get his brother out. Air crew landing at Pitomnik in mid-January had to resort to their personal weapons to fight off attempts to storm the aircraft. Now that the boot was on the other foot, General Chuikov could afford to appreciate the formidable fighting qualities of the 6th Army, noting in his account how 'up to the end of December, they continued to live in hope and put up a desperate resistance, often literally to the last cartridge. We practically took no prisoners, since the Nazis just wouldn't surrender. Not until after Von Manstein's failure to break through did morale among the German troops begin to decline very noticeably.'[40] Discipline was maintained with the same savage methods the Soviets had already resorted to. The quiet, softly-spoken Paulus had 364 of his men shot for cowardice in just one week; 18 more than Field Marshal Haig had executed in the BEF during the whole of World War I.

All able-bodied men in the pocket were combined into 'fortress battalions'. The Luftwaffe ground personnel, Flak crews, clerical staff and all rear echelon services took up rifles instead. The rapid exhaustion of medical supplies left the sick and wounded to suffer in the most revolting conditions, their numbers overwhelming the medical staff. Dysentery and typhoid fever swept through the starving units and dressing stations

DEATH OF AN ARMY

Called a 'fortress' by the German high command, the defences of Stalingrad consisted of a line of dug-outs across the bleak steppe. The Soviets found the defenders able to conduct sharp counter-attacks as late as January, but the starvation diet and lack of ammunition led to a rapid collapse once the surrender offer was rejected.

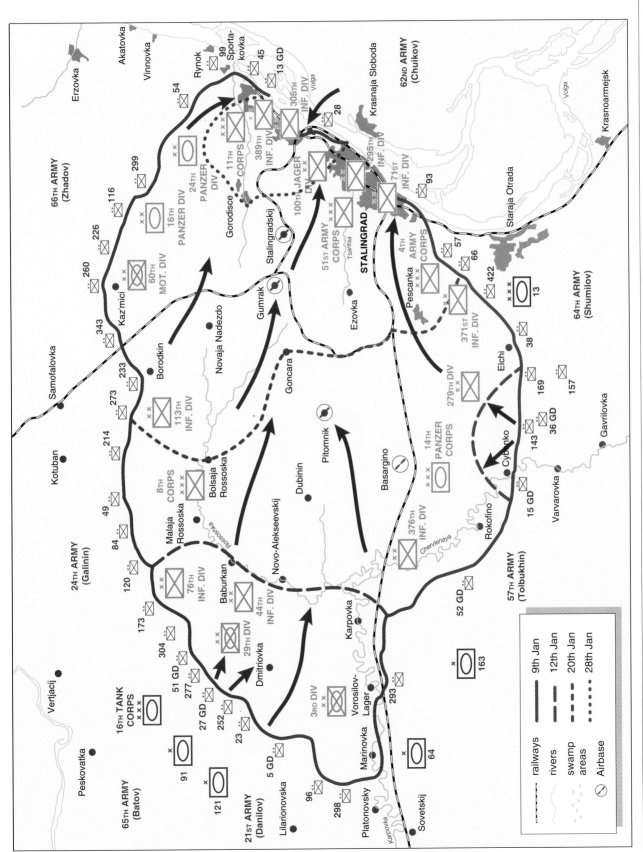

Legend:

- ——— railways
- – – – rivers
- – – – – swamp areas
- ·········· 9th Jan
- – – – 12th Jan
- – – – – 20th Jan
- ·········· 28th Jan
- ⊘ Airbase

alike. There were something like 50,000 wounded men in the pocket. Thousands had reached the field hospital at Gumrak only to be stacked into unheated freight cars at the railway station. Standing orders forbad leaving the wounded to the enemy, so as the perimeter contracted under steady Russian pressure, aid posts were cleared and the casualties moved into the city.

THE FALL OF STALINGRAD

Paulus rejected an offer to surrender on 9 January and directed that flags of truce were to be fired on in future. The next day the Russians attacked the western perimeter, where the defences, such as they were, stretched across the bare steppe. The perimeter was penetrated by tanks after a concentrated artillery barrage, and in temperatures of -30°C, the German survivors fell back towards the city itself. There was no intermediate defensive line, nothing on which to build a new position. Pitomnik airbase was overrun on 16 January, leaving the small strip at Gumrak the 6th Army's only contact with the outside world. Meanwhile, the remorseless Soviet advance to the west was capturing the airfields from which the Luftwaffe struggled to fly supplies to Stalingrad. The nearest airfield was now over 200 miles away.

On 3 March 1943 the Nazi propaganda magazine *Die Wehrmacht* carried a colour painting on its cover, showing a determined band of German soldiers led by General Karl Strecker preparing to make their last stand in the snow-covered ruins of the Stalingrad tractor factory. The reality was terribly different. The German forces in Stalingrad suffered about 60,000 casualties in December and another 100,000 in January.

LEFT *An Italian machine gun sited next to a field piece somewhere along the Don front as Operation Uranus unfolds. The Italian 8th Army was torn apart, the 2nd and 35th corps disintegrating, leaving the Alpini to fight their way out. (R. Tomasi)*

BELOW *Wearing the quilted khaki jacket introduced in 1941, Soviet infantry advance to attack. Note the compressed-felt winter boots, excellent for sub-zero temperatures. Getting frostbite was a disciplinary offence in the Red Army. (Author's collection)*

On 22 January, Gumrak - the last airfield — was overrun, a last Heinkel He-111 taking 19 wounded soldiers to safety, although its elevator was riddled by Russian ground fire as it took off. The Luftwaffe had evacuated 34,000 wounded during the siege, but that left tens of thousands of men awaiting death in conditions of indescribable horror. In the final days of Stalingrad, 6th Army signalled Army Group Don that it had so little food left, rations were no longer to be given to the wounded. The tiny quantities of sustenance available went only to the surviving fighters who continued to resist until the end, inflicting heavy losses on their attackers and even delivering counter-attacks until 25 January.

Paulus surrendered on 30 January. His forces had been split in two by the final Russian attacks, and 11th Corps, holding the Tractor factory and Barrikady ordnance works, held out until 1 February, Strecker making one last radio call. A party from 11th Corps headquarters broke out of the city as it fell, as did elements of the 71st Infantry Division and an unknown number of little groups. A few were seen by German aircraft, but were all swallowed up on the vast frozen steppe. No-one escaped alive. German aircraft flying over the city on 2 February could see no sign of movement among the ruins.

CHAPTER SIX

THE CORRELATION OF FORCES

'This war will be won by industrial production'

Stalin

In early February 1943 the survivors of the 6th Army finally crossed the Volga, not as conquerors but as prisoners. An estimated 91,000 men were still alive when Paulus surrendered, but the majority were extremely ill. Paulus himself was suffering from dysentery, which helps explain his lassitude in the final weeks. The Red Army was astonished at the number of prisoners, having grossly underestimated the size of the force trapped in the pocket. The prison camps at Beketovka and Krassno-Armiensk were swept by epidemics and as many as half the captives died from typhus, spotted fever and dysentery in the next few months – as did a number of Red Army medical staff trying to stop the spread of disease. Fewer than 6,000 men from the 6th Army would survive to return to Germany.

Hitler recognised that the Stalingrad disaster threatened the very foundations of his regime. He insisted that Paulus must fight on, promoting him to Colonel-general then Field Marshal and refusing to allow surrender. Only the renewed Soviet offensive at Christmas prevented new battalions being flown into the pocket to help the 6th Army hold out until the spring. After the last pockets of resistance had been overrun, Hitler summoned the Nazi Gauleiters to Berlin, preparing them for the news of the fall of Stalingrad. Goebbels' propaganda machine went into overdrive. Goebbels had already been reduced to faking a Christmas broadcast from the 6th Army. The radio message 'from 6th Army on the Volga' was recorded in Germany. His ministry also intercepted the last letters from Stalingrad, rightly fearing they would expose the sickening realities of *Festung Stalingrad*. Three days' mourning were declared and the radio stations played Götterdämmerung and the soldiers' lament *Ich hatt' ein' Kamaraden*.

The beginning of 1943 is a convenient moment to examine how the German and Soviet forces compared in terms of equipment, tactics, operational methods and morale, and the economic base which sustained them – what Marxist military theorists call 'the correlation of forces'.

FRONTIER ARITHMETIC

German accounts of the eastern front have developed an enduring image of massed Soviet forces bludgeoning their way west, relying on sheer weight of numbers to overwhelm the Wehrmacht. In terms of manpower, the Red Army outnumbered the invaders by a good margin in 1941, but lost so heavily in the first five months of the war (the Germans taking over 3 million prisoners by December 1941) that its rapid mobilisation barely kept pace with the losses. During 1942 the Red Army expanded at an incredible rate, and regained a substantial numerical advantage which escalated during 1944 as German forces were divided between the two fronts, and the great Soviet summer offensive tore the heart out of the Ostheer.

From the very first year of the War in the East, the Ostheer began to bleed to death, expending manpower faster than it could be replenished by the Wehrmacht's replacement system. The reserve

LEFT *It could be a scene from World War I: a German ration party makes its way forward across a moonscape of shell craters and trenches outside Sevastopol, December 1941. (Bundesarchiv)*

RIGHT *Russian Cossack volunteers of the Wehrmacht, 1943. From left to right: senior NCO, Don Cossacks; 1st lieutenant, Cossack Cavalry Corps; trooper, Kuban Cossack. Both Cossack divisions were later incorporated into the SS on Himmler's orders. Transferred to Yugoslavia to fight Tito's partisans, they surrendered to Allied forces in northern Italy in 1945. (Kevin Lyles, from Men-at-Arms 147, Foreign Volunteers of the Wehrmacht 1941–45)*

authorised number of officers in the process. The division suffered even heavier losses (nearly 17,000) in the first four months of 1945. Junior officers in the German army suffered disproportionate casualties from 1941 onwards; so bad that an infantry subaltern's chances of returning home in one piece from the Russian front compared unfavourably with those of a U-boat crewman or a fighter pilot. Command of companies frequently devolved on non-commissioned officers. Even the NCOs, the backbone of the German army, were disappearing much faster than they could be replaced.

TOTAL GERMAN STRENGTH (MILLIONS)

Date	Total	Army	SS	Luftwaffe	Navy
1941	7.3	5.2	0.16	1.5	0.4
1942	8.4	5.75	0.19	0.19	0.57
1943	9.48	6.55	0.45	1.7	0.78
1944	9.42	6.51	0.6	1.5	0.81
1945	7.83	5.3	0.83	1.0	0.7

GERMAN ARMY, AIR FORCE AND NAVY CASUALTIES 1939–45 (MILLIONS)[42]

Killed in action	1.8
Killed through other causes	0.19
Wounded	4.3
Missing in action	1.9
Total	8.19 million

pool was depleted so quickly that several emergency measures were instituted. Redefining exempt occupations released enough men for another five divisions, transferring some internal security units from Germany to the front line, and detaching one battalion each from the 23 divisions still in Western Europe at the end of 1941. Rather than reinforce the exhausted units on the front line, new formations were created, so although the total army strength in Russia increased in terms of numbers of divisions, overall manpower totals declined. In 1941 there were 3.2 million troops in 136 divisions; in 1942 there were 2.7 million men in 179 divisions. By early 1942 the Germans had lost a million men in Russia. It was only by calling up the next classes of conscripts early, substituting slave labourers for German farm workers and other expedients – as well as demanding more divisions from German allies – that the Ostheer found sufficient strength for the 1942 offensive. Hitler's lunge to the Caucasus was not only a gamble, he mortgaged the future to pay for it.

The turnover in personnel replicated the holocaust on the western front in World War I. Many German divisions lost more than their authorised strength: 18th Panzer Division had a 100 per cent turnover in enlisted men and 173 per cent in officers between June 1941 and the division's disbandment in October 1943. The famous Großdeutschland Division suffered 100 per cent casualties between summer 1942 and its retreat to the Dnepr in September 1944;[41] losing twice its

The USSR had just over twice as many men of military age as Germany, although nearly a third of the total Soviet population found itself behind enemy lines by the end of 1941. Mobilisation was ruthless, with new divisions assembled and pushed into the front line in a matter of months. Rifle battalions were filled out with older men, with teenagers serving alongside men in their thirties and forties. As the Red Army began to reconquer Soviet territory, all available men were swept into the front-line units as replacements – creating the paradox that in 1944–45, long-serving units were sometimes full of very inexperienced soldiers.

The Red Army could not have managed without the crucial assistance (deliberately played down after 1945) of Soviet women. Two million female personnel served in the armed forces. They provided most of the medical staff from base hospitals to front-line infantry companies, three-quarters of the gunners in anti-aircraft batteries defending the cities and many radio operators,

LEFT *The German army began the war with Russia highly dependent on horse-drawn transport. The situation never improved as German industry signally failed to build enough trucks to modernise the whole army. (IWM)*

including those of the partisan and special forces raiding teams. Some even served as tank crew and snipers.

SOVIET ARMY FRONT LINE STRENGTH 1941–45 (IN MILLIONS)

Jun 1941	Nov 1941	Dec 1941	Nov 1942	Jan 1944	Jun 1944	Jan 1945
4.7	2.3	4.2	6.1	6.1	6.5	6.0

Soviet army losses 1941–45 (millions)

Killed in action	6.8
Died in German captivity	2.7
Wounded	15
Sick	3
Total	27.5 million

THE BATTLE OF THE FACTORY FLOOR

The Red Army's greatest quantitative advantage lay in its vastly superior numbers of tanks, aircraft, and (above all) artillery. This was not because the USSR enjoyed greater economic resources, but because its war economy was far better managed. Despite conquering so much of Europe, Germany signally failed to exploit this industrial windfall for military production. In 1943 Germany produced about four times as much steel and three times as much coal as the USSR – after all, in 1941 it had conquered the Donbas where more than half of Russian coal was mined. Nevertheless, the Russians built 33 per cent more tanks, 50 per cent more aircraft and vastly more heavy artillery pieces. The ratio tilted sharply in favour of the Soviets during 1943–44, despite the managerial genius of 36-year-old Albert Speer who trebled German war production in three years.

Germany's only serious economic weakness was its lack of oil resources, but this had no significant impact on military production. As early as 1941 the Luftwaffe was using its reserve fuel stocks to sustain current operations, but the fuel shortages that were to dog both army and air force towards the end of the war played little part in the critical campaigns of 1942–3.

Like an army, an industrial workforce fights on its stomach. German agriculture was sustained by the increasing use of slaves, predominantly Polish and Russian/Ukrainian teenagers and even children. On Soviet farms, the ceaseless manpower demands of the front and the factories left women, children and the elderly to wrest a living from the unforgiving climate. Even a high proportion of the draught animals were taken by the army, leaving women to haul the ploughs themselves. By their largely unsung efforts, Russia had just enough to eat – the daily ration for industrial and rural workers was a quarter of the German ration and a fifth of the British.[43]

Germany had been preparing for war throughout the 1930s, and the German victories in 1940 brought the industrial resources of most of Western Europe under their control. By the time Hitler attacked Russia, half the German industrial workforce was working on military orders – a greater devotion to military production than that achieved by the USA in World War II. By every indicator of economic strength, Germany should have out-produced its opponents, enabling the Wehrmacht to face not just the Red Army but the Western Allies' invasion of France with every confidence. Had German industry been as well organised as the German army, the Allies would not have enjoyed such crushing superiority by 1944. Yet until 1943, even the much smaller British economy was out-building Germany in aircraft and warships, and closely matching its production of guns and tanks. By squandering its economic advantages in the first half of the war, the Nazi regime lost the battle on the factory floor, depriving its soldiers of the weapons and equipment they so desperately needed.

GERMAN AND SOVIET PRODUCTION FIGURES (IN MILLIONS OF TONS)

	1941	1942	1943	1944	1945
Coal					
Germany	246	258	269	281	–
USSR	151	75	93	121	149
Steel					
Germany	31	32	35	35	–
Russia	18	8	10	12	12
Oil					
Germany	6	7	–	–	–
Russia	33	22	18	18	19

THE WAR IN THE AIR

Germany used air power to devastating effect against Poland in 1939, and against Britain and France in May 1940 (indeed, it was only in the air that Germany had any superiority; in numbers of men, tanks and guns it was outnumbered). All the more astonishing then that German aircraft production remained virtually static between the outbreak of war and 1941. Throughout the Battle of Britain, the British were building more aircraft than the Germans. There was little sense of urgency demonstrated once the French aircraft industry fell into German hands. Capable of manufacturing 5,000 aircraft per year, it produced a mere 2,500 aircraft for Germany in four years of occupation – equivalent to only ten per cent of its potential, even using its relatively labour-intensive methods. Indeed, the post-war reputation of German efficiency is confounded by the incompetence with which Nazi agencies managed their conquered territories. A giant slice of Soviet industry was captured by the Germans, but only achieved ten per cent of its pre-1941 productivity under German rule. Agricultural yields in German-occupied Russia were so low (just 50 per cent of pre-1941 levels) that not enough food was produced to feed both the population and the German army – so it was the civilians who starved. For all Hitler's talk of exploiting the east, Germany received far more from Russia during the period of the Nazi–Soviet pact than it did

RIGHT *Blitzkrieg began to go wrong as early as September 1941, as German infantry divisions faced heavy counter-attacks south of Smolensk. The immense quantities of Soviet artillery reminded older officers of the western front in 1916. (Author's collection)*

after seizing most of European Russia.

Meanwhile, the Soviet aircraft industry was stepping up production. French manufacturer Louis Breguet had visited the Soviet factories in 1936, noting that 'with ten times as many personnel employed as the French, the Soviet industry is producing 20 times as many aircraft.' And the Germans knew it – a delegation of Luftwaffe officers was taken around Russian factories in April 1941. Their report, according to Field Marshal Milch, was suppressed by Göring.

AIRCRAFT PRODUCTION 1939–45
(IN THOUSANDS)[44]

Year	39	40	41	42	43	44	45
Germany	8	10	12	15	25	40	7
USSR	10	11	16	25	35	40	21
Britain	8	15	20	24	26	26	12
USA	6	13	26	48	86	96	50

The production figures conceal a second weakness of the German air arm. Under the blasé incompetence of Herman Göring, the Luftwaffe failed to develop a new generation of aircraft to replace the 1930s designs with which it won its early triumphs. Great time and effort was expended on disastrous projects like the Messerschmitt Me-210 twin-engine fighter, several manufacturers amassing fortunes but not actually delivering any new aircraft. Although some designs like the Junkers Ju-88 twin-engine bomber proved remarkably versatile, incremental improvements in veteran machines like the Messerschmitt Bf-109[45] were not enough to

match the completely new fighters of the Allied air forces. Corruption, ineptitude and the confusion of rival agencies competing for Hitler's favour left German pilots flying inferior aircraft, and the German army without air cover.

Once the Allied heavy bomber offensive against Germany gathered pace in 1943, with the first massed daylight raids by the USAAF supplementing Bomber Command's nocturnal onslaught, German production priorities changed. Interceptors were built instead of bombers, and anti-aircraft batteries concentrated around Germany's industrial cities.[46] The current *Russian school history of World War II* presents the Western Allies' strategic bombing campaign as a key factor in reducing German strength on the eastern front. The threat of an invasion of France drew most German bombers to the west at the end of the 1943, and to Italy where further amphibious assaults tempted Hitler to counter-attack.

GERMAN OPERATIONAL
BOMBERS 1943–45 [47]

	Oct 43	Dec 43	Feb 44	Jun 44	Oct 44	Dec 44
Norway	16	15	15	17	–	73
E. front	358	238	138	326	97	79
W. Europe	459	695	429	184	123	7
Italy	285	–	189	–	–	–

The Luftwaffe did make a few raids on Soviet industrial targets in 1943, but this was a local initiative by Luftflotte VI. A series of night attacks were made against the tank and engine plants at Gorky, the synthetic rubber factory at Yaroslavl and several petrol refineries in June. To put these operations into context, a total of 168 Heinkel He-111s took off to

LEFT *Russian volunteers, 1942–44. From left to right: 2nd lieutenant of an Ostbattaillon; 2nd lieutenant, possibly of the Terek Cossacks; private, Russian Liberation Army. Nearly a million former Soviet citizens joined the German forces despite the appalling behaviour of the occupation forces. A more enlightened policy might have produced enough recruits to win the War in the East. (Kevin Lyles, from Men-at-Arms 147,* Foreign Volunteers of the Wehrmacht 1941–45)

BELOW *A 1945 M4A2(76mm)W, belonging to an unidentified Soviet tank brigade. The 1st Mechanised Corps was equipped with M4 Shermans in 1945 with an IS-II heavy tank battalion attached. The 76mm-gun M4s began to arrive in January 1945. (Steven Zaloga, from New Vanguard 3,* Sherman Medium Tank 1942–45)

attack Gorky on 3 June 1943: 149 aircraft attacked and dropped 234 tons of bombs. Eight days later RAF Bomber Command attacked Dusseldorf with 693 bombers, delivering 1,968 tons of bombs in 45 minutes.

Senior Luftwaffe officers discussed transferring most of their bomber strength to strategic missions on the eastern front, but their deliberations became irrelevant as the front line was shunted westwards that summer, leaving most key targets beyond the range of German bombers. In any case, the Luftwaffe was being overwhelmed by the army's incessant demands for intervention on the front line. The German army had come to depend on tactical airpower as a substitute for heavy artillery, and as a primary element in its anti-tank defences. The escalating requirement for close air support missions that had been such a marked feature of the 1941 Blitzkrieg had never stabilised. 'Even during quiet spells, the army command insisted on the constant commitment of air power against enemy targets within the battle areas in order to conceal their own weaknesses in point of numbers and weapons.'[48]

As ground attack became the Luftwaffe's primary mission, aircraft and weapons were modified accordingly. It was not just the German army that experimented with new equipment during the battle of Kursk. The Luftwaffe introduced the Henschel Hs-129 twin-engine anti-tank aircraft, armed with 30mm guns. The Junkers Ju-87 Stuka dive-bomber also sprouted cannon. A 37mm gun

pod was added under each wing to create a formidable 'tank buster' in which Hitler's favourite airman, Colonel Rüdel, would destroy over 500 tanks. Attempts were even made to fit a Pak 40 75mm anti-tank gun to a Ju-88.

Although these flying anti-tank guns looked spectacular, the standard aerial anti-tank weapon was the SD-4-H1, a 4kg bomblet of which 78 were carried inside a 500kg bomb case. It had been learned that 250kg or heavier bombs needed to score a direct hit to knock out a tank. This was difficult to achieve, but a 'shotgun' blast of hollow-charge bomblets, each powerful enough to blow through the thin top armour, produced much better results. They were delivered primarily by Ju-87 Stukas, provided the skies were clear (if the cloud base was under 800m, the Stukas could not perform a dive-bombing attack).

In 1943 the Luftwaffe had a total strength of 6,000 aircraft of which about half were on the Russian front. Its intervention on the battlefield was enormously important, sometimes providing relatively minor operations with extremely powerful support, for instance the attack on the Soviet bridgehead south of Novorossisk in April. This involved just three German divisions, but their objective was precision-bombed by no less than 511 Ju-87 Stukas on 17 April and by 296 Ju-87s two days later. Air support was vital at the battle of Kursk, and even in the ensuing defensive battles that lasted into 1944, the Luftwaffe succeeded in making 1,000 sorties a day over critical sectors of the front.

TANKOGRAD

The German Panzer formations had achieved their great victory of 1940 by concentrating almost their entire strength on a narrow front in Northern France. Divided among three Army Groups for the invasion of Russia, and with subsequent diversions of strength to North Africa, Italy and France, Germany's armoured forces would never achieve such a concentration of strength again. Between July 1942 and March 1943, the Ostheer's monthly strength returns show an average of about 2,500 tanks in Russia, of which an average of 1,500 were operational at any one time. Over the same period, a total of 2,426 replacement tanks were shipped from Germany, 1,031 of them in the first three months of 1943 when the SS Panzer Corps was transferred from France for the Kharkov battle (see Chapter 7).

German industry was only producing enough tanks to replace its losses in Russia, but the Soviet tank forces were increasing as the relocated tank factories worked around the clock. In January 1943 German tank strength in the east peaked at 2,803[49] of which 1,475 were operational, plus about 500 Sturmgeschütz assault guns. They faced a total of 8,500 Russian tanks and assault guns[50] in five 'tank armies', backed by another 400 in Stavka reserve and 4,300 in training commands and non-operational formations. (Assault guns and tank destroyers accounted for about a third of German AFV production from 1941 to 1945, but only about a sixth of Russian AFV production.)

Labouring under the most arduous conditions, the Soviet industrial workforce – half of which was female by 1942 – forged a mighty weapon that would strike the fatal blow against Nazi Germany. In the critical year of 1943 during which the Russian army still faced the overwhelming majority of the German forces, the Russians lost four tanks for every one German tank destroyed, but the factories more than made up for the losses.

Total German tank strength (all fronts) 1943–45[51]

	Jan 43	Jul 43	Jan 44	Jul 44	Jan 45
PzII	1,000	200	400	450	n/a
PzIII	2,950	1,300	900	800	510
PzIV	1,100	1,400	1,700	2,400	1,800
PzV Panther	0	450	1,200	2,250	2,150
PzVI Tiger	60	260	410	670	280
PzVI Tiger II	0	0	0	60	190

German tank losses (all fronts)

	1943	1944
PzIII	2,633	220
PzIV	2,396	3,103
PzV Panther	493	2,803
PzVI Tiger I	291	788

Armoured vehicle production

	1940	1941	1942	1943	1944	1945
Soviet	2,794	6,590	24,446	24,089	28,963	15,419
German	2,200	5,200	9,200	17,300	22,100	4,400

Soviet production after 1941 concentrated on only four types of armoured vehicle: the KV-1 heavy tank, T-34 medium tank and the T-60 and T-70 light tanks. From 1943 the light tanks were

LEFT *German army divisions found themselves struggling to defend wide frontages with inadequate artillery and anti-tank support. The Luftwaffe became wholly devoted to missions within the battle area, its Junkers Ju-87 Stuka divebombers playing a prominent role. (R. Tomasi)*

RIGHT *Soviet troops captured at Kharkov in the early summer of 1942. Stalin had insisted on pressing home this disasterous attack: its failure left him more disposed to trust the professional judgement of his senior officers. (R. Tomasi)*

finished as self-propelled guns instead (the SU-76) and the above-detailed totals include 19,000 self-propelled guns built from 1942 to 1945. (An additional 1,200 or so self-propelled guns were created by fitting 76mm guns onto captured German tank chassis, mainly PzKpfw IIIs and StuG IIIs.) T-34s made up the overwhelming bulk of Soviet AFV production – of the 24,000 vehicles built in 1942, only 2,553 were KV-1s.

If the enormous disparity between Soviet and German production seems bad enough in 1942 (a ratio of more than 2.5:1), it is important to note that the situation never really improved. The figures cited above – and usually given as 'tank' production in most reference books – actually include all manner of self-propelled guns, ammunition carriers, self-propelled anti-aircraft guns and other specialist vehicles. The totals for tank, self-propelled gun and assault gun production are far lower:

German late-war tank production [52]

1943	1944	1945
11,667	13,109	1,836

The Panzer divisions were hopelessly outnumbered. Nevertheless, they and the German anti-tank gun batteries exacted a very high price, destroying Soviet tanks at the following rates:

Russian tank losses

1941	1943	1944
22,600	22,400	16,900

Of these, about 66 per cent were destroyed in action: the rest were lost to mechanical break-down. Soviet figures reveal that of tanks knocked out in battle 10 per cent could be repaired by the unit, 15 per cent could be repaired at Russian factories, and 75 per cent were beyond repair and their crews killed or wounded.

A tank – and in most cases its crew – had a life expectancy of about six months between leaving the factory and destruction in battle. Frequent German remarks about the poor standards of Soviet tank crew (driving along crests, poor co-ordination with friendly infantry) testify to the difficulty of learning by experience with such a high turn-over of personnel.

The Russians subordinated almost every aspect of weapons design to the dictates of mass production. They standardised wherever possible, concentrating on two main types of tank (the T-34 and KV-1) a handful of artillery pieces, one principal rifle and one primary sub-machine gun. The latter typifies the Soviet approach: the PPSh-41 looks ugly, feels poorly-balanced when you pick it up, and its accuracy is unexceptional. On

ammunition ducking to avoid the breech of the 76mm gun. Its tracks were not rubber clad: this, and its unmuffled diesel, made it one of the loudest tanks ever to rumble into action – in its own way a psychological weapon, like the Stuka dive-bomber's siren (although it had one disadvantage; the engine needed about 30 minutes to warm up, giving audible warning to the Germans that the T-34 was on its way). All Russian tanks had wide tracks to reduce their ground pressure and give better grip on snow or muddy surfaces. Their cross-country performance was superior to the Panzer III or IV.

Although improved by the substitution of an 85mm gun for its 76mm weapon, the T-34/85 was still greatly inferior to the famous German PzKpfw V, or Panther. Introduced in 1943, the Panther had a superb ballistic shape, a high-velocity 75mm gun, powerful engine and even infra-red sights by 1945, but it was hideously complex to build and maintain. Flung into battle at Kursk, before troop trials could be conducted, the Panther proved superior in tank v. tank engagements, knocking out T-34s at over 3,000 meters, although fuel pump failures and motor breakdowns (the engines had not been run in) put about a third of them out of action after a few days' fighting. The Panther was a magnificent design but Germany could only build a few hundred a month – whereas T-34s were coming out of Tankograd (Chelyabinsk) at a rate of nearly 2,000 a month.

In April and May 1944, production of the famous PzKpfw VI Tiger I peaked at 100 vehicles per month. With its 88mm gun, thick armour, and

the other hand, the inside of its barrel is beautifully chromed so it is not corroded by mercury-primed ammunition that will function at -50°C. It is strong enough to batter down doors or enemy soldiers without damaging the weapon, and it keeps firing in snow, sand, grit or mud. As for accuracy, as one German veteran commented, in close quarter battle one should shoot first and aim later.

The T-34, often cited as the best tank of the war, was crudely-finished too, its turrets rough cast. There was no turret floor, and the loader's life was a hazardous one as he (or she) scrambled around for

wide tracks for good cross-country performance, the Tiger trumped any other tank on the battle-field, but it had a desperately short range which led some infantrymen to prefer to be supported by the more common Sturmgeschütz, which did not disappear to refuel just when you needed it most. The Tiger was also too heavy for German army bridging equipment and permanent bridges tended to collapse under its weight, further reducing its operational effectiveness.

To compensate for its lack of armour, the German army improvised an incredible variety of tank destroyers, which were issued to the anti-tank battalions of Panzer and Panzer Grenadier divisions. Obsolete French and Czech tanks formed the basis for many conversions. The turret was removed and a more powerful anti-tank gun substituted in an open mounting with limited traverse. German tank chassis were used too, some to create formidable tank killers with enclosed fighting compartments, low silhouettes and powerful guns. Production totals of the main types were as follows:

Total	Type
132	Panzerjäger I (47mm gun on Panzer I chassis)
1,217	Marder II (75mm gun on Panzer II)
799	Marder III (75mm gun on Skoda THNP-S/Panzer 38(t))
2,500	Hetzer (full conversion of Panzer 38(t) with enclosed fighting compartment)
473	Nashorn (88mm on Panzer IV chassis in open compartment)
90	Panzerjäger Tiger (P) Elefant (88mm Pak 43 on Porsche Tiger chassis)
1,000	Jagdpanzer IV (75mm gun on Panzer IV chassis with enclosed compartment)
382	Jagdpanther (88mm on Panther chassis in enclosed compartment)
77	Jagdtiger (128mm gun on Tiger II chassis)

The Germans also developed a bewildering variety of self-propelled guns, mounting field guns and howitzers on just about every type of tracked vehicle they had captured from the French in 1940. The introduction of so many types of vehicle (all in small quantities) made their logistic difficulties even worse, but it was a case of impro-vise or die. Some were used only for indirect fire, but others, like the Brummbär, were designed for direct support of the infantry. Production totals for the main types were as follows:

Type	Total
schwere Infanterie Geschütz 33 (150mm howitzer on Panzer I chassis)	370
Wespe (105mm howitzer on Panzer II chassis)	c.700
Hummel (150mm howitzer on Panzer IV chassis)	c.750
Brummbär (150mm howitzer on Panzer IV enclosed compartment)	313
Sturmtiger (380mm rocket projector on Tiger I chassis)	c.10

Often used in a similar role, and as a substitute tank, the Germans also came to rely on the Sturmgeschütz assault gun. Almost as many of these were built as all the other conversions combined. Pre-war plans called for each infantry division to receive a six-gun battery of assault guns which mounted a short 75mm gun on the hull of a Panzer III, but there were only three or four such batteries ready for the 1940 campaign. By 1941 there were eight 28-gun battalions and a number of independent nine-gun batteries in service. A total of 642 Sturmgeschütz III (with 75mm L/24) built between 1940 and 1942 were still in service in July 1942 when production switched to a new version with the 75mm L/48, offering much greater anti-tank capability. The short-barrelled StuG III disappeared during 1943, but assault gun battalions with the 75mm L/48 were widely employed, one or two being attached at corps level. Favoured divisions – especially the SS Panzer and Panzer-grenadier formations – had integral Sturmgeschütz battalions. Production totals were as follows:

Type	Dates	Total built
StuG III (75mm L/24)	1940–42	822
StuG III (75mm L/48)	1942	699
StuG III (75mm L/48)	1943–44	3,000
StuG IV (105mm L/28)	1943	300
StuG IV (105mm L/28)	1944	900

In 1943 Germany built 2,663 StuG IIIs and they seemed to have lasted longer at the front. Between September 1943 and May 1944 the Ostheer had more operational StuGs than tanks: average tank strength was 433 vehicles, average assault gun strength was 661. Why the Sturmgeschütz provided so high a proportion of the armoured forces is not clear, but it was more mechanically reliable (no turret to go wrong) and German doctrine called for the StuGs to operate only with close infantry support.

The Russians appreciated the value of self-propelled anti-tank guns too, introducing three dual purpose assault gun/tank destroyer vehicles in the summer of 1942. The SU-76 combined a 76mm gun in an open mounting on a T-60 or T-70 light tank chassis, while the SU-122 was a 122mm howitzer on a T-34 chassis. The self-propelled gun regiments created late that year had four batteries of SU-76s (four guns each) and two of SU-122s (four guns each). In early 1943 the regiments were reorganised and consisted of either 21 Su-76s or 16 SU-122s. The first SU-152 (152mm guns on a KV-1 chassis) regiment was

ready for the battle of Kursk that July. Some SU-122s carried 122mm guns rather than howitzers. The SU-85 and SU-100 carried 85mm and 100mm anti-tank guns respectively and were intended to counter the new German heavy tanks. Production totals were as follows:

Type	Total built
SU-76	14,000
SU-85/100/122	4,000
SU-122/152	5,000

By mid-1944 each Russian tank and mechanised corps had one light, one medium and one heavy self-propelled gun regiment and there were many independent SP gun regiments (241 by 1945). Light regiments had five batteries of four SU-76s; medium regiments had four batteries of four SU-85/100/122; and heavy regiments had five batteries each of two SU-122/152s.

AMERICAN AND BRITISH AID

At fearful cost in sailors' lives Britain provided the USSR with military aid, beginning as early as 1 August 1941 when HMS *Abdiel* delivered mines to the Soviet Northern Fleet. The Royal Navy escorted convoys of Allied merchant ships through the Norwegian and Barents seas to Murmansk and Archangel. The arrival of German surface units, from destroyers to heavy units like *Admiral Scheer*, *Scharnhorst* and eventually *Bismarck*'s sistership *Tirpitz* as well as a substantial number of U-boats led to a new naval war in the world's most

dangerous waters. These convoy battles are a story in themselves.[53] Some British leaders like Field Marshal Lord Alanbrooke doubted their value, believing the sacrifice of men and *matériel* was unjustified from Britain's point of view. It was certainly unappreciated. Soviet leaders took their cue from Stalin and kept up a steady stream of invective. They criticised the rate of delivery (4,000 tanks in 1942 from Britain and America, equivalent to just 16 per cent of Soviet production for that year) and affected not to understand the fearsome difficulties of fighting a convoy through the Arctic in the teeth of Luftwaffe air attack, U-boat assaults and occasional sorties by German battleships.

Between 1941 and 1945 Britain and America supplied the following totals, of which about 75 per cent of British aid arrived via the Arctic. Most US aid was despatched via Iran or the Pacific. Britain supplied 5,218 tanks,[54] 7,411 aircraft, 4,932 anti-tank guns, 473 million rounds of ammunition, 4,338 radio sets, 1,803 radar sets, ten destroyers, and one battleship. The USA supplied 7,537 tanks, 14,795 aircraft, 51,503 jeeps, 375,883 trucks, 1,981 railroad locomotives, 11,155 railroad wagons, 2.6 million tons of gasoline, 3.7 million tyres, and 345,735 tons of high explosive.

Stalin and his commanders knew they were being ungenerous. Perhaps it stuck in the throat to accept aid from the very Allied powers (and in the person of Winston Churchill, the same leader) that had landed military forces at the same ports – Murmansk, Vladivostock – in 1919 to crush the Bolsheviks in the Russian Civil War. The great

RIGHT *Lend-lease in evidence, September 1943; two knocked-out British Valentines and a T-34D. Soviet crews disliked the British tanks' narrow tracks but praised the reliability of the engines. (Author's collection)*

BOTTOM *Cossack cavalry draw their sabres for the cameras, September 1942. In snow, forests and swamps on the Russian front, cavalry proved more mobile than motorised vehicles. (R. Tomasi)*

tank armies with which the Red Army broke the back of the Wehrmacht in 1944 depended on American trucks to carry their supplies of fuel and ammunition. Their artillery and supporting weapons as well as accompanying infantry were also truck-mounted.

Allied tanks were quickly introduced to Russian armoured units, with the first British tanks seeing action as early as January 1942. However, since half the Allied tanks supplied to the Red Army arrived in 1944–45, the critical battles of 1942–3 were fought almost entirely with Soviet vehicles. Those tanks that did arrive were distributed widely: in the summer of 1943, a quarter of all Russian tank brigades had some Allied tanks on their strength. British tanks had narrow tracks, unsuitable for snow or mud, but were prized for their excellent engines, which outlasted those of Soviet tanks, making them ideal for training. Soviet tanks were not built to last, but they were usually destroyed in battle before their engines gave out. However, low standards of production and mainte-

nance led to heavy losses from mechanical breakdown especially during 1941–2.

For the sake of simplicity, the Soviets asked the British to supply only Valentines from 1942, and the production line was kept open for the Red Army – all 1,388 Valentines built in Canada were shipped to the Red Army. American tanks were disliked because of their gasoline-powered engines and tendency to brew up.[55] Just as British tank crew dubbed the American M4s the 'Ronson' (because it lights every time), so Russians christened the M3 Lee tank the 'coffin for seven comrades'.

HORSES v. STUDEBAKERS

The addition of several hundred thousand American trucks gave the Red Army's armoured forces new strategic mobility. At the same time, the Wehrmacht found itself relying more and more on draught animals. Tanks, trucks and self-propelled guns were concentrated in a few elite units which spearheaded every offensive or rushed to block each Soviet attack. But the rest of the German army underwent a demoralising process of 'de-modernisation', fighting an increasingly well-equipped enemy with much the same weapons as their fathers on the western front between 1914 and 1918.

German infantry divisions had more automatic weapons than their First World War equivalents, but fewer field guns. From 1942 many divisions were reorganised with six battalions rather than nine, but although their firepower was augmented with extra machine guns and mortars, especially captured Russian 120mm weapons, Germany was unable to substitute technology for manpower. German artillery relied on experienced forward observers and well-trained crews to deliver 'time-on-target' concentrations of fire that partially compensated for their numerical inferiority. Against comparatively inexperienced Soviet artillery units, this worked well into 1944 but over time the Russians learned, while Germany failed to solve its production problems and German tactical airpower had become no more than a memory.

Even the Panzer divisions were not immune to this process, and their experience was arguably the more traumatic as heavy losses in their tank regiments left some of them as little more than motorised infantry brigades with a dozen or so tanks in support. For instance, only a few weeks after the invasion of Russia the 18th Panzer Division had just 12 operational tanks left. By November 1941 Panzergruppe Guderian had no more than 150 tanks out of the 1,150 it had employed since 22 June. Many Panzer and Panzergrenadier divisions endured a horrific cycle of attrition that saw them reconstituted after near annihilation, only to be overwhelmed again.

SS UNITS ON THE RUSSIAN FRONT

The SS evolved into a state within a state. From one of the armed wings of the Nazi party, it grew into an army, industrial conglomerate, internal security agency, eugenic breeding system, and, above all, perpetrator of the most notorious act of genocide ever committed. Its military role on the eastern front became crucial, the SS armoured divisions Leibstandarte, Das Reich, Totenkopf and Wiking playing the leading role in both Manstein's counter-attack at Kharkov and the last

great German offensive at Kursk. The political clout of the SS ensured these divisions secured the lion's share of new equipment, and their authorised strengths were larger than that of their Wehrmacht equivalents.

The SS more than trebled in size from 1942 to 1944, but of the 450,000 SS men serving in 1943, only a small proportion were in the well-known Panzer-grenadier formations. Only one new SS division (9th Hohenstaufen) was formed in 1942[56] and that did not see active service until early 1944 when committed to Poland. The combat record of the elite SS Panzer formations was excellent by any standards. However, there was a widespread conviction within the German army that these ideological shock troops suffered excessive casualties through foolhardy displays of National Socialist ardour. Worse, the diversion of so many troops to 'ethnic cleansing' seems especially perverse in the face of Germany's manpower crisis. By 1943 there were more men serving in the Einsatzgruppen than were lost with the 6th Army at Stalingrad. Towards the end of the war, only about half the enlisted SS personnel were German. A quarter were ethnic Germans from conquered Europe and a quarter were foreign volunteers.

Power politics among the Nazi leaders led to further profligate use of German manpower. Rather than turn over personnel to the army as was suggested at the end of 1942, Göring insisted on following Himmler's example and having an

LEFT *A Sturmgeschütz assault gun under evaluation by the US Army after the war. Manned by artillerymen and with fewer working parts to go wrong, by late 1943 StuGs out-numbered tanks in the Ostheer. (US Army)*

BELOW LEFT *The Ostheer's lack of tanks was not because German armour was concentrated elsewhere. In secondary theatres like the Yugoslav guerrilla war, obsolete tanks (like this captured French H.39/40) were pressed into service. (R. Tomasi)*

army of his own. Twenty Luftwaffe field divisions (each of two regiments of three battalions with a total authorised strength of 9,800) were eventually formed. They were poorly-trained and required a steady infusion of officers and NCOs from the regular army to keep them operational. Again, German army officers were appalled at how these divisions sustained unnecessary losses because their bravery was not allied to tactical proficiency.

THE PARTISAN WAR

In the summer of 1942 Himmler appointed his adjutant SS Gruppenführer Knoblauch as chief of the Reichsführer SS command staff, with special responsibility for countering the Soviet partisans. The army's nine security divisions (formed of six or seven battalions of old soldiers and equipped with obsolete weapons) were clearly inadequate to police the occupied territories. Although the combined strength of these units, the Einsatz-gruppen and the *ordnungspolizei* (regular police) exceeded 100,000 men by the end of 1941, they had some 850,000 square miles to control. In August 1942 the term 'partisan' was replaced by

'bandit' in SS documents, signalling an even more brutal phase in an already ghastly campaign of terror and counter-terror. Mass killings of civilians in retaliation for attacks on the German forces (a hundred shot for the death of one German) were supplemented by indiscriminate slaughters. Many 'anti-partisan' operations presented the '6,000/480 problem': 6,000 Russians were killed but only 480 weapons captured. German losses might be less than half-a-dozen, sometimes there were none. These were outright massacres without regard to the age or sex of the victims. Children as young as ten were regularly tortured and shot as spies. The incredible brutality was documented in nauseating detail by some German troops (regular army as well as SS) with their personal cameras – for all the wrong reasons.

The Russian revolution and the civil war had seen some hideous acts of cruelty by Russians against 'class enemies' of their own nationality and other ethnic groups. Indeed, the Jews of Kiev (see Chapter 3) had endured a terrible pogrom at the hands of the White Army.[57] So the peoples of the occupied territories were not slow to respond to German atrocities and began executing captured Germans in the most revolting ways imaginable. During 1942 the partisans began to conscript people into their ranks, and sometimes resorted to terror tactics against the population too, forcing men to join and holding their families hostage. At the same time the Germans began to round up able-bodied men and women for forced labour in the Reich (children under 15 years of age had to be abandoned to starve when villages were cleared). This stampeded more people into the forests, swelling the ranks of the guerrilla bands that grew to over 100,000 strong by the end of the year. As in 1941, the open spaces of the Ukraine were least affected by partisan action while about half the guerrillas were established in the trackless forests of Belorussia.

Elements within the German army and SS favoured the recruitment of local troops to counter the partisan threat. Hitler remained utterly opposed to the idea of Russians wearing his uniform, but other national groups (like the Cossacks) were acceptable to him. Nevertheless, over a million Russians did serve the German army. The service troops that made up to ten to 20 per cent of divisional strengths were supplemented by an eventual total of 176 Ostruppen battalions, 150,000 men by mid-1943. Some 180,000 men were recruited into the UNS (Popular Self-Defence Corps) in the Ukraine for security operations. Many Ostruppen units were transferred to France and Italy on Hitler's orders, stimulating the desertion that their removal from Russia was supposed to prevent. The UNS and Russian auxiliary police units retreated westwards from 1943 as the Germans were driven back, many of their personnel being absorbed into the SS.

Perhaps the most notorious counter-guerrilla formation was that led by a former Soviet officer, Bronislaw Kaminski. He led a force of five regiments, including 20 T-34 tanks, against the partisans south of Bryansk until the German defeats at Kursk and Orel in the summer of 1943 left his fiefdom menaced by the Red Army.

Kaminski's 'Russian National Liberation Army' (RONA) was displaced westwards, a force totalling 50,000 people including the soldiers' families. In May 1944 he was appointed SS Oberführer and his followers became 29th SS Division 'RONA'. His renegade army later took part in the suppression of the Warsaw uprising, where its pitiless savagery beggars description. Kaminski was murdered by some SS men for reasons that remain obscure, his death faked to appear the work of partisans and the unit passed to another Russian, a former lieutenant called Belai.

That the German forces could recruit more than a million Russians to their colours despite all the atrocities and the deportations suggests that the Nazi racial policies brought about their own defeat. As many senior figures (even Goebbels by

LEFT *The Soviet regime appreciated that farm and factory workers were as critical to victory as soldiers. Close relations were fostered between all three. Here, workers from the Moscow Farmers' Commune hand over KV-1C heavy tanks, which they have helped to finance. (Author's collection)*

BELOW LEFT *Panzer Grenadiers peer up at the sky in the Belgorod–Orel battles of 1942. The Soviet air force had only limited impact until 1943, but low level attacks against German artillery positions proved difficult to stop. (R. Tomasi)*

1943) came to believe, had the Germans behaved with even a modicum of humanity, a great many Russians would not just have accepted German rule but actively fought alongside the German army against the Communist regime. Of course, by the time Goebbels came around to this view, it was too late. Soviet citizens knew exactly what kind of rule they could expect if Germany won the war. And after two years of being encouraged

to commit all manner of cruelties on 'Bolshevik sub-humans', casual brutality had become so ingrained in the Ostheer that units transferred to other fronts would sometimes lapse into old habits – as massacres of Allied prisoners in the Normandy campaign and the Battle of the Bulge would demonstrate.

By mid-1943 when the partisan war was at its height, approximately 250,000 partisans were in the field, with perhaps 500,000 men (army, SS, police and security units) ranged against them. On the eve of the battle of Kursk, and again as the great summer offensive of 1944 began, the partisans launched concerted attacks against rail communications. This exacerbated German logistic difficulties and tied down even more personnel guarding the trains, bridges, water-towers and other facilities. After 1945 it was claimed that the partisans killed tens of thousands of German soldiers and had played a decisive part in the Soviet victory, but OKH sources record only about 15,000 casualties attributable to the guerrillas. Compared to the enormous body counts racked up on some counter-guerrilla sweeps in Belorussia, this ironically reinforces the impression that such operations were more concerned with 'ethnic cleansing' than the pursuit of military objectives.

Given the suspicion with which Stalin's secret police regarded anyone who had been the wrong side of the lines during the war, millions of Soviet citizens had a keen personal interest in exaggerating their contribution to the war. There are obvious parallels with the exponential rise of resistance groups in France after June 1944. In fact, the partisans diverted large numbers of second-grade troops to security operations and certainly undermined German efforts at several critical points, but they did not play a decisive role. Some areas of northern and central Russia were effectively in Soviet control although behind the German lines (Luftwaffe maps showed in red those areas over which it was dangerous to fly and suicidal to land) and as an eventual Soviet victory looked likely, so these areas expanded. Yet the Baltic States remained free of partisan activity, as did all of the Crimea except the mountains along its southern shores. The steppes of the Ukraine gave little cover for guerrilla bands, and attempts to initiate partisan action were frequently defeated. Although powerful guerrilla bands were formed in the Ukraine, they were fighting for independence and vigorously resisted the Soviet army in 1944 – Marshal Vatutin himself being killed – and they would carry on the fight well into the 1950s.

THE FAILURE OF BLITZKRIEG

The defeat of the German 1942 offensive revealed the limitations of Blitzkrieg. It did not have universal application. The substitution of air-power for artillery, and the mechanisation of a dozen divisions had enabled Germany to beat France. But the events of 1940 were as much the consequence of French political and military errors as anything else. The German army staked everything on another rapid victory in 1941, and when this failed, tried a second Blitzkrieg in 1942, this time aimed at economic as much as political objectives. Enormous distances were covered in both campaigns, but the German army could not affect a truly strategic breakthrough. Its great battles of encirclement were not, proportionately, as significant as the complete rupture of the Allied front achieved in 1940. The ratio of 'force to space' was simply inadequate. Having failed to deliver a knock-out blow, the German army found itself embroiled in a *materialschlacht* very like that of 1914–18 – worse in fact. In World War I Russia sent soldiers into battle without rifles, hoping they would pick up weapons discarded by casualties. This time, Russia was out-producing Germany.

Accustomed to short victorious wars, German soldiers were neither physically nor psychologically prepared for this return to trench warfare. They were used to living in centrally-heated barrack blocks, not squalid holes in the ground. 'Despite the heavy emphasis on marching, hiking and field exercises, there had been entirely too

LEFT *The comparatively poor performance of German industry led the German forces to adopt a staggering variety of captured military vehicles, requiring vast quantities of non-interchangeable spare parts. Here an ex-French army Chenilette Lorraine has been pressed into service as an artillery tractor. (US National Archives)*

BELOW LEFT *Public hangings were carried out by the German army from the first weeks of the campaign. The idea was to terrify the conquered population into submission. But such repressive measures stimulated the guerrilla opposition they sought to discourage. (Author's collection)*

The battlefield performance of the Red Army improved by fits and starts, not least because Stalin ordered operations beyond its abilities in both 1941 and 1942. The combination of over-ambitious offensives that produced sharp defeats and the enduring legacy of the purges, inexperienced officers and a culture of fear that discouraged initiative concealed the great strengths of the Soviet military. Its operational philosophy was far more realistic than that of OKH, matching its resources to the scale of the front. It emphasised artillery firepower, integrating aerial bombing with the artillery fireplan, primarily in counter-battery work, attacking German gun positions and employing its tank formations to exploit to great depth. As soon as Soviet factories had provided the tools, the Red Army put its pre-war theories into practice. The result was the 1944 offensive, Operation Bagration in which the Soviet army attacked and destroyed the main body of the German army, effectively winning World War II before the Allied divisions landed in Normandy had managed to break out from the beaches.

Eighteen months earlier, as the fight for Stalingrad ended and the Soviets tried to bounce the German army out of Kharkov, Zaporozhe and the Dnepr crossings, the ultimate triumph of the Russian army lay in the future. At the beginning of 1943, the overwhelming majority of the German army was still concentrated on the eastern front. And as the Soviet South-West Front was about to discover, it was still man-for-man, battalion-for-battalion the most deadly military instrument in the world.

much stress laid upon nearly a "peacetime" type of garrison life which bore little resemblance to the stark and foreboding realities of life on the eastern front … In Russia, German troops were required to live for long periods of time in the open, in all kinds of weather, often in vermin-infested bunkers or redoubts where clothing changes could seldom be made … the German soldier and airman, resting on an impressive string of victories, was soon provided with a number of startling surprises in Russia, almost all of them bad.'[58]

CHAPTER SEVEN

THE LAST BLITZKRIEG

*'Anyone who speaks to me of peace without victory
will lose his head, no matter who he is.'*

Adolf Hitler

Just a week after the surrender of Stalingrad, Soviet armoured forces were thundering across the open steppe south of Kharkov, heading for Zaporezhe. This was not just a key crossing point over the Dnepr but the site of a gigantic hydro-electric plant recently repaired by AEG to provide power to neighbouring factories and coal mines. The Russians were racing against time: the spring thaw would soon impose a halt to mobile operations. As the snow fields melted, the roads would become swamps, as would the surrounding fields where soldiers' lives would be more miserable than usual – supplies could not come in nor wounded men be taken out as fighting continued in a sea of mud.

In fact the weather was not the only menace looming over the Voronezh and South-West Fronts. In Zaporezhe, Field Marshal von Manstein had taken charge and was planning a counter-stroke that would confirm his reputation as one of the greatest commanders of World War II. But first he had to confront the Führer.

Hitler had already despatched his Praetorians to rescue the eastern front. The SS Panzer-grenadier Divisions Leibstandarte (92 tanks), Das Reich (131 tanks), and Totenkopf (121 tanks) formed the SS Panzer Corps – and Wiking division was already in action south of Kharkov. The SS were ordered to hold Kharkov, which would have suited the Russians who were preparing to by-pass the city and snap up any garrison at their leisure. On 14 February, the SS abandoned Kharkov, local resistance fighters sniping at their rearguards as they departed.

Kharkov was the first major Soviet city to be recaptured from the Germans. A largely Ukrainian city, with a population of 900,000 in 1940, its heavy industry (tank and tractor factories) had been evacuated in 1941. Occupied for 18 months by the Germans, its fate provided chilling evidence of what German rule meant for ordinary Russian and Ukrainian people – let alone for Jews. The Red Army estimated that only 350,000 people remained in Kharkov in early 1943, about

RIGHT *Leningrad's terrible ordeal ended in January 1943. The 2nd Shock Army attacked on the Volkhov front as the garrison attacked across the frozen River Neva. In a week of heavy fighting, a land corridor was established along the southern shore of Lake Ladoga. Here, Soviet cameras record the meeting in Leningrad of soldiers from 2nd Shock with men from the 67th Army. (Novosti)*

SUMMER 1943

Both sides attacked in 1943. The Soviets followed up their victory at Stalingrad by pressing as far west as Kharkov, but the city was retaken during Von Manstein's celebrated counter-attack in February. The German generals then planned to attack the salient around Kursk, but the operation was delayed until July. Marshal Zhukov banked on stopping the German assault, then launching offensives of his own both north and south.

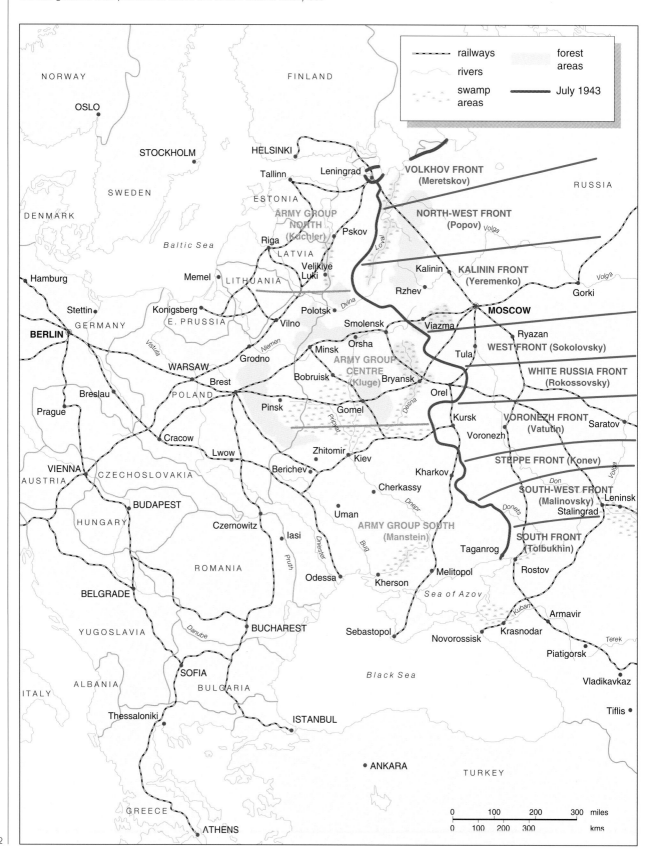

Legend:
- ━·━·━ railways
- ∿∿ rivers
- ∴∴ swamp areas
- ▒ forest areas
- ━━━ July 1943

half the population left in the city when the Germans took over. Where were the rest? It was soon established that over 100,000 young men and women had been deported to Germany as slaves. Almost as many, the old and the very young especially, had died of malnutrition, hypothermia and related conditions. Most deaths occurred during the winter of 1941–2, but the enduring food shortage had contributed to another sharp rise in mortality in the four months before liberation. About 30,000 individuals were spared the horrors of the starvation winter. The Germans killed about 15,000 Jews and a similar total of Communist party members, Soviet officials, intellectuals (most teachers at the university) and prisoners-of-war shortly after they took over.

The German occupying authorities created a desperately transparent 'Ukrainian' regime in Kharkov, seeking to divide Ukrainian from Russian. A local Ukrainian police force was established, the usual band of looters, racists and psychopaths that graced many a German-occupied city in Eastern Europe during World War II. There was a Ukrainian *burgomeister* who fled Kharkov with his fellow Quislings, mistresses and booty as the Red Army approached. As in the Reich itself, Nazi rule did not just bring the worst elements in society to the surface, it empowered them. Men who belonged behind bars were instead given uniforms and guns. In Kharkov the schools were shut down, but the black market flourished. Luxurious restaurants catered for the Germans who also helped themselves to everything from watches to women.

LEFT *Routine maintenance on a Panzer III. Germany began 1943 with more tanks on the eastern front than at any time since the invasion; a total of 2,800, although only half were operational. In February the Ostheer lost over 1,000 tanks: this proved to be its heaviest monthly loss until September 1944. (Author's collection)*

BELOW LEFT *As the spring thaw melted the snow in the southern Ukraine, the Germans were in full retreat. An attempt was made to hold the line of the River Donets, and retain the industries of the Don basin. Stalin however was pressing his generals to break through to the Dnepr. (R. Tomasi)*

The brief return of Soviet administration to Kharkov was marked by several unpleasant features that would appear on a greater scale in 1943, as more Soviet territory was recaptured. With sinister congruence, the NKVD took over the former Gestapo headquarters and used the same basement torture chambers. Letter boxes were added to the building so the citizens of Kharkov could denounce collaborators – or settle old scores that might have little to do with the occupation. Again, the war and the Nazi/Soviet political systems had a deeply corrosive effect on humanity. Among the beggars seen near the market by British correspondent Alexander Werth were former prisoners-of-war from a camp outside the city. Most of their fellow POWs had died of starvation before the camp was 'liberated', but neither the Red Army nor the people of Kharkov would feed them. They were regarded with callous indifference, except by the NKVD which treated them as spies or traitors.

Their tragedy anticipated a greater manifestation of Stalinist evil that would follow the final victory. In May 1945 Stalin ordered 100 prison camps to be built by his armies in Germany and Poland,[59] into which were driven hundreds of thousands of bewildered Soviet soldiers who had survived capture by the Germans. Most were catapulted from German POW camps to Soviet ones, and thence to the GULAG. Only about one man in five ever returned home.

Hitler was so furious at the continuing success of the Soviet offensive that he flew to Zaporezhe himself, where the conference was held to the accompaniment of the distant rumbling of Russian guns. Colonel-general Popov's 'mobile group' (four Soviet tank corps) continued to attack although it was at the extreme limit of its supply lines and short of fuel and ammunition. Elements of the 25th Tank Corps were within ten miles of the city, but the tank corps had only 53 operational tanks between them.[60]

Manstein stood up to Hitler and was allowed to conduct a mobile battle instead of the sort of static defence the Führer tended to insist upon. The over-strength SS formations were backed by five Panzer divisions (3rd, 6th, 7th, 11th and 17th) as well as the Großdeutschland division (95 tanks). Popov's communications were being monitored by the Luftflotte IV which learned of his logistic problems and concentrated its efforts against the Soviet spearheads. As the weather improved, the Luftwaffe supported Manstein's counter-attack with up to 1,000 sorties per day. Popov's units

were pounded by Junkers Ju-88s with little interference from the Soviet air force.

The Soviets were gambling. The Russian armoured forces were running way ahead of their supply lines, hoping to capture the Zaporezhe crossings and cut off all German forces between the east bank of the Dnepr and the Black Sea. Instead, the Germans' mobile defensive tactics lured them to their destruction. Manstein's timing was perfect. The Soviet formations that had broken across the Donets and nearly reached the Dnepr between Zaporezhe and Dnepropetrovsk were cut off and eliminated. Ordered to keep attacking despite the menace to their flanks and their mounting losses, the two Fronts were torn apart by a concentrated German tank attack delivered in the old style. The SS Panzer Corps led the advance back to Kharkov, which it recaptured by a frontal attack in mid-March. Soviet losses were estimated at 23,000 men, 615 tanks and 354 guns although many soldiers abandoned their vehicles and equipment to escape back to Russian lines. Only 9,000 prisoners were taken.

At the height of the Donets campaign, Army Group Centre was under attack too. Since the spring thaw spread from south to north, operations here went on for several weeks before the mud arrested progress. Airpower was again vital in stabilising the front, and although Velikie-Luki could not be saved, the Soviets were prevented from breaking through to Orel: on 18 March the Luftwaffe

destroyed 116 Russian tanks. The Soviet offensive was halted, but only after it had driven a deep wedge into the German front. This unsightly bulge – the Kursk salient – was immediately earmarked for destruction by OKW. Eliminating it would drastically shorten the frontage German forces had to defend, and would remove the obvious platform for the Soviets' summer offensive.

The incredible recovery in the Wehrmacht's fighting power from the Stalingrad debâcle to the triumphant return of the SS to Kharkov was a profound shock to Stalin. There is some evidence that the Soviet leader toyed with offering a compromise peace to Germany, using Swedish diplomats as neutral intermediaries.[61] The deal apparently involved a return to the borders of 1914, not 1941. Stalin's creation of the National Committee for Free Germany and the League of German officers was an insurance policy intended to lay the ground for a military coup in Berlin. If Hitler was not prepared to negotiate, then perhaps his generals would be more open to reason. However, those senior German commanders contemplating action, like Von Kluge who gave his blessing to two attempted assassinations of Hitler in 1943, sought to make peace in the west in order to continue the War in the East. Ironically, this fantasy would later be shared by many senior Nazis as the Red Army approached the frontiers of the Reich.

Of course, Hitler had no thoughts of compromise. Resorting to increased doses of dubious medicines, containing strychnine and atropine, prescribed by his sinister physician Dr Morrell, the Führer spoke of destiny and final victory. The rock upon which German strategy rested – or foundered – was Hitler's 'unconquerable will'. Anything that might weaken this, such as the clinically accurate assessments of Colonel Gehlen's *Fremde Heer Ost*, was simply ignored.

THE BATTLE OF KURSK

Strategies for 1943 were guided by the fact that the Soviets enjoyed a 2:1 advantage in manpower, and an overwhelming superiority in artillery and tanks. In the spring of 1943 comparative strengths on the eastern front were as follows:

	German	Soviet
Men	2.7 million	6 million
Tanks	2,209	12–15,000
Field guns	6,360	33,000 [62]

Nearly half the German infantry divisions were reduced to six battalions, with their artillery

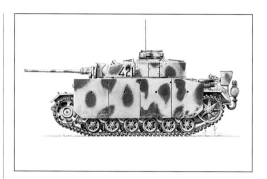

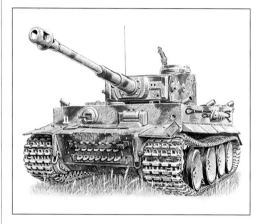

batteries cut to three guns. Reinforced on the eve of the Kursk offensive, the Ostheer would have about 2,500 tanks of which 90 per cent were operational. The Russians' front line tank strength seems to have hovered around 8–10,000, with large quantities of vehicles either in reserve formations or training. Since few Russian tank crew survived the loss of their vehicle, the Red Army had to provide new crews with replacement tanks. The daunting quantities of Soviet guns had now received American trucks to tow them, substantially improving their mobility.

The attack on Kursk was to have been followed by a German offensive in the north, code-named Operation Parkplatz, which was intended to take Leningrad by storm. Given the extraordinary losses suffered by the 6th Army at Stalingrad in October 1942, it is astonishing that Hitler still had any appetite for warfare in built-up areas. Nine divisions were earmarked to join Army Group North for the assault, although Field Marshal von Küchler signalled that he had enough siege artillery in place and would not require more. In the event, the failure at Kursk and the Soviet breakthrough at Orel led to the cancellation of the attack. The siege of Leningrad, which had already cost the lives of over a million people by 1943, would not be completely lifted until 1944.

The first operational order for the Kursk offensive was issued in March 1943. The resultant

plan called for Army Group Centre (Field Marshal von Kluge) to attack the north flank of the salient using the German 9th Army (12 infantry and four Panzer divisions), Kampfgruppe Esebeck (two Panzer divisions) and with 5th and 8th Panzer Divisions in Army Group reserve. The 2nd Army would hold the face of the salient with just two corps of three infantry divisions each. Army Group South (Field Marshal von Manstein) would assault the southern flank with the 4th Panzer army (10 infantry, four Panzer and five Panzer-grenadier divisions) plus the (re-constituted) 6th Army (including one Panzer-grenadier division) and Armeeabteilung Kempf (including nine divisions).

The attack was postponed several times to allow the new battalions of Tiger tanks and the first Panthers to take part. The idea that an offensive involving millions of men fighting across a battlefield half the size of England could be determined by a few hundred new tanks shows touching faith in technology. The 147 Tigers performed well, but the 200 Panthers were reduced to 50 by the end of the second day. Their engines had not been run in and inevitable mechanical problems dogged Panzer Regiment 39 for the duration of the battle. It fell to those workhorses of the Wehrmacht, the Panzerkampfwagen III and IV to provide the bulk of the German army's tanks at Kursk. The 16 Panzer and five Panzer-grenadier divisions taking part in Kursk included a total of 115 Panzer IIs, 844 Panzer IIIs, 913 Panzer IVs and some 300

TOP LEFT *A 1943 PzKpfw III Ausf.M, belonging to 3.SS-Panzer-Division 'Totenkopf'. The scheme is taken from a photograph probably dating from the battle of Kursk in July. (David Smith)*

LEFT *A 1943 Tiger E, of 8/sPzKp, 2.SS-Panzer-Grenadier-Division 'Liebstandarte Adolf Hitler', typical of those which saw action at Kursk. Tigers formed less than five per cent of the German tank force at Kursk. Großdeutschland Panzer-grenadier Division and the SS Panzer Divisions Leibstandarte, Das Reich and Totenkopf each having a single company of 13 or 14 Tiger Is. Three-quarters of the German tanks at Kursk were PzKpfw IIIs or IVs. (David Smith)*

BOTTOM *SS-Gruppenführer Paul Hausser ignored a direct order from Hitler and abandoned Kharkov, enabling the SS Panzer Corps to survive and take part in Von Manstein's brilliant counter-attack in February 1943. Here the 1st SS division LSSAH celebrates its return to the city in March. (Author's collection)*

StuG III assault guns. SS Das Reich even had 25 captured T-34s.

Delaying the attack gave the Russians ample opportunity to fortify their positions in the salient, and they did so with typical thoroughness. Prodigious quantities of mines were laid – over 3,000 per km – and up to eight successive lines of defences bristling with anti-tank weapons awaited the German onslaught. Significantly, the Soviet high command was already planning its own offensive against the Orel salient on the assumption that the German attack on Kursk would be defeated. The odds were certainly unfavourable to the Germans:

	German	Soviet
Men	600,000	1.2 million
Tanks and assault guns	2,750	3,500
Guns and mortars	10,000	25,000

Estimates of the German ground forces range from 435,000[63] to the more usually quoted 900,000. The larger figure includes German forces which, strictly speaking, did not take part in the Kursk fighting, such as six divisions of the German 9th Army engaged in the fighting around Orel which began a week after Kursk, but which were not involved in the original German offensive. The commonly quoted figure of 1.3 million Soviet troops[64] is the sum of the Central and Voronezh Fronts' ration strength, as understood after the war, but recent Soviet sources put this at nearer to one million. However, this total does not include the 5th Guards and 5th Tank Armies of Konev's Steppe Front, which were brought forward to block the southern thrust of 4th Panzer Army. Konev's Front had nine infantry and one airborne divisions plus five mechanised corps and a tank brigade including 1,500 tanks and self-propelled guns. Its total strength was about 500,000 but only part of the Steppe Front counter-attacked at Kursk: the rest took part in the subsequent Soviet offensive.

This suggests that about 600,000 German soldiers were attacking about 1.2 million Soviets in the battle for the Kursk salient. If, like Soviet historians, you look at the operations that July from Orel to Belgorod, the Soviet Bryansk Front and elements of the West Front should be added to the Soviet order of battle, giving more Germans to over 1.5 million Russians. In both cases the figures reflect the overall Soviet advantage in manpower of over 2:1.

On the northern side of the salient the German 9th Army commanded by Generaloberst Model faced the bulk of the Soviet Central Front under General Konstantin Rokossovksy, a half-Polish former Tsarist officer who had survived torture and imprisonment during the purges, and was released in early 1940. Rokossovsky had served in the Far East under Marshal Blyukher. Whether the dismal Russian performance in Finland or signs of renewed trouble with Japan triggered his release is unknown, but Timoshenko

had no hesitation in giving him back his old job as commander of a cavalry corps. Promoted to command the new 9th Mechanised Corps, Rokossovsky survived the Kiev encirclement in 1941, his candid account of that disaster proving too much for the Soviet regime as late as 1984.[65] At Stalingrad Rokossovsky had commanded the Don Front, retitled the Central Front in February 1943, and had been preparing to defend the Kursk salient for nearly four months.

The Germans had so telegraphed their intentions that Rokossovsky was able to order a bombardment of Model's start line two hours before the German offensive began. Nevertheless, the German artillery opened fire at 4.30 a.m. It was a short but intense bombardment, planned for maximum shock effect, with the Luftwaffe joining in after 40 minutes (730 aircraft from Luftflotte VI) and the ground forces commencing their assault under cover of both air and artillery bombardment. Accounts of the battle of Kursk have often focused on the new heavy tanks employed by the Germans. Model's assault was led by the most exotic combination: 89 Elefant assault guns of schwere Panzerjäger Abteillung 656, together with the 31 Tigers of schwere Panzer Abteillung 505 were used to spearhead the assault, supported by the 45 Brummbär assault guns of Sturmpanzer-Abteillung 216. Their extremely heavy armour made them a tough proposition for the Soviet anti-tank weapons, and they made the initial penetration. Only one of Model's Panzer divisions

(the 20th) took part in the first day's fighting: the other five were ready to pour through once a gap had been blown in the Soviet defences.

The Elefants suffered from a lack of defensive machine guns (a problem the Sturmgeschütz battalions had already addressed) and lost some of their number to Soviet infantry anti-tank teams. Many of the Tiger Is were disabled by mines, and their commanders complained that they were asked to do too much. However, Model's plan worked. The battalions of heavy tanks led the infantry through the first line of Soviet field works, and smashed the Soviet counter-attack into the bargain. On 5 July, Model's 9th Army advanced about 4 miles against the Russian 13th Army. The Russian 2nd Tank Army counter-attacked, but suffered such terrible losses that Rokossovsky sacked its commander, Lieutenant-general Rodin. Rokossovsky ordered the surviving Russian armour to be dug in among the defensive positions and not to attempt to fight a mobile battle.

Now the Panzer divisions poured into the gap, ready to slash through the remains of the defences and break into open country. Between the small towns of Ol'hovatka and Ponyri, ten infantry and four Panzer divisions battered their way forward, but there seemed to be no end to the Russian defences. Fighting from deep entrenchments practically impervious to artillery fire, the Russian infantry kept firing, reducing German infantry companies to mere handfuls of men. Although the German tanks

LEFT *The men of the SS Panzer Corps were equipped with reversible parkas ideal for the freeze/thaw conditions of the Ukraine in early 1943. (Author's collection)*

BELOW *Taking aim with an MP40 during the street fighting in Kharkov. In close quarter battle, SS men were taught instinctive shooting techniques: as one veteran commented, 'shoot first, aim later'. (Author's collection)*

RIGHT *German troops near Orel, late March 1943. The fighting here led to the creation of a massive salient around Kursk. (Author's collection)*

BOTTOM *SS Panzer Grenadiers outside Kharkov. By insisting on continuing the offensive, Stalin played into Von Manstein's hands and exposed his forces to a devastating counter-attack. (R. Tomasi)*

were knocking out impressive numbers of Soviet vehicles, they were suffering steady attrition themselves, especially track damage caused by land mines. Soviet engineers laid another 6,000 mines on Rokossovsky's front during 6 July alone. They rarely knocked out German tanks, but often put them out of action for vital hours. Prodigious quantities of ammunition were expended, German veterans remembering the unceasing fire of the Soviet artillery. And although the Soviet air force was losing heavily in the battles overhead, Soviet fighter–bombers persisted in making low level sorties against German artillery positions – coming in under the German radar coverage and attacking before they could be intercepted.

Model's army never did break into the open. After a week of intensive fighting, day and night, his divisions had advanced about six miles. On 12 July, the Soviets launched Operation Kutuzov, an attack on the Orel salient which forced Army Group Centre onto the defensive. The ground won at such bitter cost was abandoned as Model turned his forces to face the new threat.

Army Group South had more armour than Army Group North, with 13 Panzer and Panzer-grenadier divisions including the SS Panzer Corps

as well as the 200 Panther tanks of Panzer Regiment 39. The Großdeutschland Division and the SS divisions LSSAH, Das Reich and Totenkopf each had a company (13–15 tanks) of Tigers while schwere Panzer Abteilung 503 had 45 Tigers. The Army Group was supported by 1,100 aircraft assigned to Fliegerkorps VIII.

The planner of the Sedan breakthrough and recent victor at Kharkov, Field Marshal von Manstein conducted his assault very differently from Model, attacking with massed armour from

the very first hour. The 4th Panzer Army under the veteran tank commander Generaloberst Hoth broke into the Soviet defences north-west of Belgorod under cover of an equally short but sharp artillery bombardment. The Soviet 6th Guards Army could not stop the onslaught. General Vatutin, commander of the Voronezh Front, brought forward the 1st Tank Army (6th and 31st Tank Corps) with both his reserve Tank Corps (2nd and 5th Guards), a total of over 1,000 tanks to block the approaches to Obajan.

The city of Belgorod lies on the west bank of the Donets, and was just within German lines at the southern neck of the Kursk salient. The German Armeeabteilung Kempf (six infantry and three Panzer divisions plus three assault gun battalions) had succeeded in bridging the river and establishing a bridgehead, but the forewarned Soviet artillery battalions delivered an intensive barrage just as the Germans tried to break out. Nevertheless, German engineers laid two more bridges south of the city and by noon on 5 July, the Panzer divisions were crossing the Donets, poised to sweep along the east bank, guarding the flank of Hoth's Panzer Army as it headed for Kursk.

Whether Vatutin or his tank commanders were aware of the fate of the 2nd Tank Army's counter-attack in the north, or were simply more cautious, the 1st Tank Army did not launch itself at Hoth's Panzers. A counter-attack scheduled for 6 July was cancelled and the Soviet tanks took up defensive positions behind the infantry, the anti-

LEFT Waffen-SS troops in Russia, 1941–43. From left to right: SS-Reiter, SS-Kavallerie-Div.; SS-Schütze, infantry; SS-Uscha., infantry. The SS cavalry was primarily employed on 'ethnic cleansing' operations dressed up as anti-partisan sweeps. Thousands of Russians were killed, but few weapons recovered. SS casualties were tiny until the division served in the frontline as part of 9th Army. (Jeffrey Burn, from Men-at-Arms 34, The Waffen-SS)

BELOW SS Das Reich in action on the Donets, April 1943. Two Soviet armies had to be sent to reinforce the front north of Kharkov as the German counter-offensive continued. (R. Tomasi)

RIGHT *SS Panzer Grenadiers take a break during the battle of Kursk. Hoth's 4th Panzer Army demonstrated exceptional professionalism, attacking the heavily-fortified Soviet positions, breaking through and taking on substantially larger Soviet armoured forces.* (R. Tomasi)

BELOW RIGHT *A Panzer III at an SS headquarters at Kursk. The spaced armour protected its sides and turret against hollow-charge anti-tank rounds.* (R. Tomasi)

tank guns, anti-tank ditches and minefields. The 1st Tank Army was on high ground overlooking the River Ps'ol, south-west of Obajan; the 2nd and 5th Tank Corps were behind the 69th Army to the south-east. In reserve 150km further east lay the 5th Guards Tank Army of Konev's Steppe Front. If Hoth led 4th Panzer Army directly for Kursk, he would run into 1st Tank Army and leave his right flank exposed to the rest of Vatutin's armour, and 5th Guards Tank Army. Instead, Hoth veered north-east, towards the small town of Prochorovka where the Belgorod–Voronezh road intersects the Kursk–Belgorod railroad. Advancing in this direction also avoided further bridging operations. Hoth would pass between the Ps'ol and the headwaters of the Donets. Given the German dependence on heavy tanks that were too large for standard army bridging equipment, this was no small consideration.

The 4th Panzer Army crashed through the Soviet defences with incredible skill and élan. Against the most formidable entrenchments, stubbornly defended, the 48th Panzer Corps and II SS Panzer Corps advanced 30km in a week to reach a line running from Verhopen'e, along the high ground towards Prochorovka. At Verhopen'e, combat engineers repaired the bridge and the Großdeutschland Division rolled up the defences, taking numerous prisoners from the 71st Guards Rifle Division. The II SS Panzer Corps broke through to the west of Prochorovka. On its left, Totenkopf established a bridgehead over the Ps'ol on 11 July. For seven days, Stalin, Zhukov and

Vassilevski monitored the progress of the battle – demanding hourly reports on 10 and 11 July. They were determined to preserve as large an operational reserve as possible, ready for their own offensive. The German attack in the north had been stopped without recourse to massive reinforcements, but 4th Panzer Army was still grinding its way through one defensive line after another. The Soviet 69th Army, in danger of being cut off between Hoth's Panzers and Armeeabteilung Kempf, was compelled to withdraw.

The 5th Guards Tank Army (18th and 29th Tank Corps plus 5th Mechanised Corps) was transferred to Vatutin's operational control on 9 July and ordered, as Hoth had predicted, to Prochorovka. The 5th Guards Army was despatched too, occupying the 45km front between Obajan and Prochorovka on 11 July. The 5th Guards Tank Army counter-attacked on 12 July together with 2nd Tank Corps and 2nd Guards Tank Corps from Steppe Front's reserve. A

murderous, chaotic tank battle ensued to the dramatic background of a summer storm as II SS Panzer Corps continued to attack as well.

The same day Field Marshals von Kluge and von Manstein were summoned to Hitler's head-quarters. A tense meeting ensued on 13 July. The British and Americans had landed on Sicily and Italian forces were offering little resistance. Army Group South was ordered to despatch II SS Panzer Corps to Italy, in the expectation of an attack on the mainland. Operation Citadel was cancelled.

The battle of Kursk was hailed as a great victory in Russia and Stalin ordered a triumphal salute to be fired in Moscow. The Red Army had received the most powerful blow the German army could deliver, parried it, and commenced two major offensives of its own. In the chaos of a great tank battle – as in an aerial dogfight – exor-bitant numbers of 'kills' tend to be claimed. At Kursk they were inflated out of all proportion, with claims of hundreds if not thousands of tanks destroyed. The Soviets claimed to have destroyed 2,952 tanks and 195 assault guns, killed 70,000 men and shot down 1,392 aircraft at Kursk.[66]

These bogus figures have become part of the legend, the presentation of Kursk as a mortal blow to the German army in general and the Panzer divisions in particular. Army Group Centre reported the loss of nearly half its tanks; a total of 304 written off including 39 of the Elefants. Army Group South lost a total of 233 tanks completely destroyed during Operation Zitadelle, including 58 Panthers. (One of the unforeseen problems with the Panther was that it took three SdKfz 18t half-tracks to tow one damaged Panther, hence the large number that had to be blown up and abandoned.) By the end of July Army Group South had about 500 operational tanks; roughly half as many as it began the battle with. Assuming losses among the Sturmgeschütz battalions were in proportion, Operation Citadel cost the Germans between 600 and 700 tanks and assault guns. Yet German tank strength on the eastern front was approximately 1,500 at the beginning of 1943 and remained level at about 2,000 through the whole year, although operational readiness was seldom more than 50 per cent and often lower.

The Panzer divisions were not wiped out at Kursk, and neither was the Luftwaffe. In the skies above Kursk the Luftwaffe once again shot down vast quantities of Soviet aircraft for little loss: 432 Russian aircraft were shot down on the first day for 23 German. For the German fighter arm, flying on the eastern front was regarded as opera-tional training. Although several famous German aces served there for years, amassing enormous scores in the process, the majority of fighter pilots committed to Russia were transferred to defence of the Reich as soon as they had gained enough combat experience. They were replaced by newly-trained pilots straight from training establishments. However, the Luftwaffe discovered that its bombers could no longer beat off Soviet fighter attacks unaided. Even the Heinkel He-111s, which had hitherto relied on close formations and relatively good defensive firepower, had to be shielded by Me-109s. Soviet fighter operations continued to improve, with British radar sets arriving in sufficient quantities to give GCI coverage of the whole front by early 1944.

The exploits of the Ilyushin Il-2 Sturmovik have dominated coverage of the eastern front air war, but in 1943 it was the success of the fighters – La-5s, Yak-7s and Yak-9s especially – that had greatest impact, substantially reducing the number of effective German bombing missions. The

Sturmoviks made regular attacks against German ground forces, but suffered dreadful losses both to fighters and Flak, once the latter were issued with armour-piercing ammunition. The fact that the position of rear gunner in an Il-2 was a punishment posting, to which flight crew were sent for disciplinary offences including cowardice, says much about the Red Army's confidence in its ground attack aircraft. The Il-2's main contribution seems to have been to blind Luftwaffe reconnaissance. It could overtake and shoot down the Fw 189s of the German recce flights, confident its frontal armour would protect it from the German rear gunner.

OREL, KHARKOV AND THE RETREAT TO THE DNEPR

The Soviet drive on Orel involved the Western and Bryansk Fronts in a similar grinding battle of attrition to which the German armoured forces had been committed at Kursk. The German defences were thoroughly prepared, and if they now lacked massive tank reserves with which to restore the line, the Luftwaffe proved an effective substitute for both artillery and anti-tank guns. The 9th Army and 2nd Panzer Army defending Orel were aided by 37,000 sorties, with many aircraft flying five or six missions per day. The 1st Air Division delivered some 20,000 tons of ordnance, claiming 1,100 Russian tanks and 1,300 other vehicles destroyed. The Russian air force was still inferior, losing 1,733 aircraft over the Orel front to a total of only 64 German aircraft.[67]

Try as they might, the German forces were unable to stop the Soviet offensives. Although the Ostheer exacted a heavy and unceasing toll of casualties for every position it had to abandon, the front line was driven steadily westwards. The Soviet attacks were supported by intensive artillery barrages that demolished all but the most thoroughly-constructed positions, and the forces engaged at Kursk were still full of fight and able to mount an offensive of their own. By 5 August the Soviet 3rd Guards Tank Army had captured Orel and two weeks later, the Briansk salient had been overrun. Model withdrew to the 'Hagen' line of fortifications, built a few miles east of Briansk roughly along the line of the highway running north–south of the city.

A new Russian attack south of Kursk smashed through the German defensive lines to take Belgorod on 5 August and fight another major tank action with the 2nd and 3rd SS Divisions on the outskirts of Kharkov.

Manstein fought (and lost) the fourth and final battle for Kharkov in August 1943, arguing that it was essential to retreat to a solid defensive line before winter. After a series of meetings with his senior commanders on the eastern front, Hitler was eventually persuaded to allow a withdrawal to the River Dnepr. Supported by the greater share of Luftwaffe resources (750–1,000 sorties per day, half of them bomber missions), Army Group Centre gave ground slowly against repeated Soviet offensives. The Soviet Western and Kalinin Fronts eventually recaptured Smolensk in early

again. The savagery of the German army in retreat had already been a feature of the War in the East. When the Wehrmacht fell back in winter 1941 it had destroyed what it could not take with it. Deportations and outright massacres of civilians had accompanied all subsequent withdrawals, a policy for which Field Marshal von Manstein and other senior army officers would be brought to trial after the war.

While not seeking to excuse the actions of some units, the German army had practically abandoned all judicial process by 1943. The court martial system was frequently bypassed and soldiers simply shot out of hand. Rule of law was replaced by terror. Over 15,000 military executions were carried out by the German army in World War II, almost all on the Russian front. With the Russians on one hand, partisans itching for revenge, and their own officers increasingly ready to resort to the pistol, it is small wonder that some German soldiers were driven to excessive violence against those least able to defend themselves.

Even more grotesque activities began behind the front line. In August 1943 SS Standartenführer Paul Blobel, former commander of Sonderkommando 4a, returned to Babi Yar (see Chapter 3) with his new unit Sonderkommando 1005. His task was to destroy the evidence of mass murders before the areas were overrun by the Soviets. Three hundred prisoners-of-war were used to disinter the bodies, pile them on improvised grates (the iron gates from the local cemetery), soak them in

September, but at a terrible cost. The South-Western and Southern Fronts drove back Army Group South to prepared defensive positions running from Zaporezhe to the Black Sea, and succeeded in isolating the Crimea, occupied by the German 17th Army.

The German army conducted an intensive 'scorched earth' policy as it fell back towards the Dnepr. In many villages every building was destroyed. This was nothing new, it had been standard operating procedure for the Ostheer, but it was carried out by soldiers with the increasing suspicion that they would never be passing this way

gasoline and burn them. The bones were ground up with iron rollers, mixed with sand and scattered in the fields. When the job was done, the prisoners were ordered to fire up the grates once more, then the SS men shot them and disposed of their bodies the same way – except that one group of prisoners made a run for it when it became obvious what was about to happen.

The retreat was not only marked by German atrocities. The Luftwaffe methodically blew up airfield facilities, cratering runways and then sowing them with SD-2 pressure mines to prevent the Soviets using them. The practice was abandoned when it was discovered that the Russians were marching German prisoners-of-war across the runways to detonate the bombs.

Soviet mechanised forces reached the Dnepr either side of Kiev in late September, but an attempt to storm the river crossings at Kanev and Bukrin (90km downstream) using three airborne divisions met with bloody defeat. One division was parachuted directly on to the positions of the 10th Panzer Grenadier division, which Soviet intelligence had not located. A bridgehead was established at Bukrin, but sealed off by the Germans. A month later, the 3rd Tank Army and 7th Artillery Breakthrough Corps abandoned the bridgehead, crossed back to the east side of the river and headed north. Their radios remained behind still broadcasting, so its arrival in the tiny west-bank foothold at Lyutlezh, 20km upstream of Kiev, came

as a very disagreeable surprise. On 3 November, the German infantry divisions hemming Lyutlezh were struck by a hurricane bombardment from 2,000 guns, mortars and rocket launchers: 300 tubes per km of front! The 3rd Tank Army overran the defences and surged towards Kiev, which the Germans evacuated three days later.

LEFT *An SS anti-tank gun waiting for the next Soviet assault, September 1943. The shortage of anti-tank guns compelled the ground forces to rely on air support to stop Soviet breakthroughs. (IWM)*

The Voronezh Front surged west another 100km to take Zhitomir and Korosten before Manstein counter-attacked with the 48th Panzer Corps in mid-November. The core of the force consisted of the 1st and 7th Panzer Divisions, SS Division Leibstandarte Adolf Hitler and the 68th Infantry Division, plus the weakened 19th and 25th Panzer divisions and a Kampfgruppe made up of the survivors from 2nd SS Division Das Reich. The Germans recaptured both towns and re-established the direct railroad link with Army Group Centre. A more ambitious counter-stroke, aimed at attacking Kiev from the south-west and cutting off a large proportion of the Voronezh Front was abandoned in favour of an almost frontal attack. Generalmajor Mellenthin blames Generaloberst Rauss, the commander of 4th Panzer Army for excessive caution here.[68] However, Konev's Steppe Front stormed the German defences on the Dnepr further south and captured Cherkassy in early December. German forces still held the river line between the original Soviet bridgehead at Bukrin and the city of Kiev, but were becoming dangerously exposed to an encirclement. While vainly continuing his counter-attack towards Kiev, Manstein repeatedly requested permission to evacuate this dangerous salient. Hitler contented himself with the sacking of the outstanding tank commander General-oberst Hoth.

CHAPTER EIGHT

THE WRITING ON THE WALL

*'The policy of clinging on at all costs in particular places
repeatedly changed the campaign for the worse'*

General Dittmar

RIGHT *A Panzer III
churns up the snow,
winter 1943. Soviet
bridgeheads on the west
bank of the Dnepr
continued to expand in
early 1944, but Hitler
insisted on holding an
exposed salient around
Korsun, south of Kiev.
(IWM)*

During their counter-attacks around Zhitomir in November, the Germans took several thousand prisoners-of-war, but most were either young teenagers or older men, some in their fifties. It seemed that Russian manpower was not inexhaustible after all, a revelation that, as Mellenthin observed, 'strengthened our determination to stick it out'. Indeed, the authorised strength of a Russian rifle division had been reduced twice during 1943, the numbers of replacements were insufficient to sustain existing units, even when newly-liberated villages and towns were combed for young men to fill out Soviet units.[69] The Germans regarded the Russian infantry division of late 1943 as only half as capable as that of mid-1942. Nevertheless, the Russians had enough infantry, even of reduced quality, and morale was high. Desertion rates were now a quarter of what they had been in the summer. The Red Army now included an incredible number of guns, rockets and mortars – 80 artillery and mortar divisions in addition to organic heavy weapons of the infantry and tank units. There were five tank armies, and a sixth was created in January 1944. The correlation of forces by the end of 1943 was very unfavourable to the Germans:

	German	Soviet
Men[70]	2.5 million	6 million
Tanks and SP guns[71]	1,500	5,600
Guns and mortars[72]	8,000	100,000
Aircraft[73]	2,000	13,000

The quantities of armoured vehicles listed here are total strengths, the number of operational German vehicles was even smaller. The same applies to the 2,000 Luftwaffe aircraft on the Russian front: no more than 1,500 were serviceable, and most of the aircraft were transport, liaison, trainer or obsolete types. There were just 385 German fighters (301 operational) in the east

and 238 bombers. The Germans had an additional 706,000 men, the armies of their various allies, but very few of them fought effectively in 1944. By the same token, the Germans had stationed disproportionately large forces in Finland, the 20th Mountain Army expanding to 176,000 men. By the end of 1943 this was about the only German army with its infantry divisions at full establishment, but the Finns refused to hazard another offensive against the Russians, or even declare war on the USA. They were looking for a way to end their part in the war.

'LITTLE STALINGRAD'

In February 1944, a year after the remnants of the 6th Army surrendered at Stalingrad, Hitler engineered a similar disaster, albeit on a smaller scale. The Führer temporarily forsook his headquarters in East Prussia for his beloved Berghof. Camouflage netting blotted out the celebrated alpine views, but there was an ominous glow on the northern horizon where RAF Bomber Command was attacking Munich. German forces still held a section of the west bank of the Dnepr between Kanev and Cherkassy. The 52nd Corps (1st Panzer Army) defended the northern sector, but it was being outflanked. The Soviet bridgehead around Kiev, 80km upstream, extended

Konev launched a full-scale offensive on 24 January, 4th Guards Army and the 5th Guards Tank Army attacking from the south-east. German resistance was extremely determined, and the assault made little progress despite very strong artillery support. However, General Kravchenko's newly-formed 6th Tank Army broke through in the north to link up with Konev's troops on 3 February. The two German corps were trapped in an oval-shaped 'pocket' extending east–west 100km from the high ground[74] around Medvin and Korsun'-Shevchenkovsky to Cherkassy, and north–south 40km from the River Rossava to Gorodishche. The 11th Corps consisted of the 57th, 72nd and 389th Infantry divisions, but they lacked anti-tank weapons and only the 72nd was strong enough for offensive operations. The 52nd Corps had the 88th and 112th infantry divisions, 5th SS Panzer division Wiking and the Belgian volunteer brigade Wallonien.[75]

The commander of the trapped forces, General Werner Stemmermann conducted a staunch defence, having stockpiled supplies in expectation – duly proved correct – that air supply would be inadequate. The Soviet air force concentrated its fighters over the pocket, and deployed several flak divisions along the path of German transport aircraft. A Russian lieutenant-colonel arrived on 9 February to offer terms, was treated to a glass of champagne and sent on his way. One of the German commanders captured at Stalingrad, General von Seydlitz, wrote to at least one officer in the pocket suggesting he follow the example of the nineteenth-century Prussian hero Yorck, who went over to the Russians in the war of 1812.

westwards despite the counter-attack described above. By the end of December 1943, the Corps was bent back to hold an east–west front line just north of Boguslav. Vatutin's 1st Ukrainian Front (formerly the Voronezh Front) continued attacking from this direction during January, driving the Germans back to the River Rossava. The area around Cherkassy was defended by the 11th Corps (German 8th Army), but this now formed the southern side of a salient extending back westwards to Lys'anka, the Soviet 2nd Ukrainian Front under Konev steadily lapping around it. All the evidence pointed to a potential encirclement, but Hitler adamantly refused to allow a timely withdrawal.

DECEMBER 1943

The battle of Kursk did not destroy the German armoured forces as is often alleged. Losses were far heavier during the long retreat across the Ukraine in the autumn, with large numbers of vehicles abandoned in the mud. The Soviet advance reached as far as Zhitomir before Manstein's counter-attacks drove them back again, but the recapture of Kiev proved impossible.

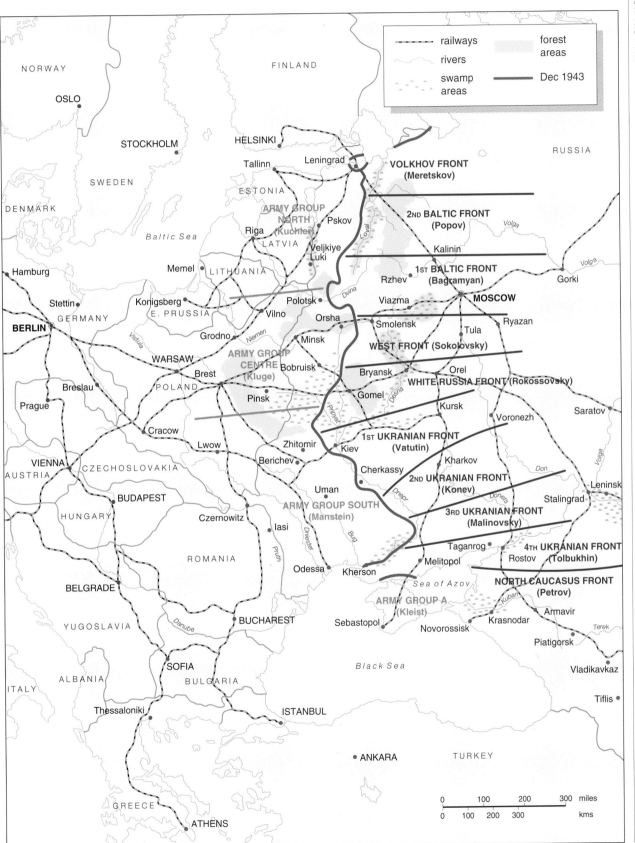

Field Marshal von Manstein counter-attacked with the 3rd Panzer Corps (1st, 16th, 17th Panzer divisions plus 1st SS Panzer Division LSSAH). On 11 February the Germans crossed the River Gniloy Tikich but were unable to expand their bridgehead. Ironically, it was unseasonable warm weather that was the problem. Unusually warm days alternating with the normal winter cold turned the unmetalled roads into a glutinous mass. Soviet tanks, with their wider tracks and lower ground pressure could cope with the conditions rather better. Their more homogenous wheeled transport (mainly American) was also more able to keep moving than the bizarre collection of lorries operated by the Germans.

By 15 February it was clear that the relief force was spent. It could hold its ground, but further progress was impossible. Stemmermann would have to break-out. The weather closed in, grounding the Luftwaffe but not the Soviets. Konev found volunteer pilots in U-2s to locate and bomb the village of Shanderovka where Stemmermann's survivors were assembling for a 'do or die' assault in the morning. They ignited enough fires to guide in more bombers and provide a marker for the Soviet artillery.

The encircled German troops formed up in two columns to fight their way across the 16km separating Shanderovka from the River Gniloy Tikich and safety. The retreat began and ended with a grisly massacre. Setting out into a snowstorm on 17 February, the Germans blew up all immobilised vehicles and heavy guns for which there was no ammunition. They shot their wounded in the back of the head ('as they usually shoot Russians and Jews' as one Soviet officer noted) and 'in many cases they set fire to the ambulance vans with the dead inside. One of the oddest sights were the charred skeletons in those burned-out vans, with wide bracelets of plaster-of-Paris round their arms or legs. For plaster-of-Paris doesn't burn …'[76]

Progress was deceptively easy for the first few miles. Then the Soviets attacked with tanks and mounted cavalry and the columns were split into pieces. The German units dissolved into a mass of fugitives, and they were hunted down and slaughtered without mercy. Several desperate bands broke through to the river at Lys'anka, including a couple of tanks which were lost trying to ford it (the river

RIGHT *German airborne forces were expanded as the war continued. Apart from a few minor operations, they were only employed as ground troops. These paratroops are in the southern Ukraine, March 1944. (IWM)*

BELOW *A StuG and several half-track armoured personnel carriers cross the featureless steppe, winter 1943–44. The counter-attack to relieve the Cherkassy pocket failed, leaving the encircled troops to break out on their own. (Author's collection)*

was about three metres deep). As the Soviets realised how many Germans had reached the bank, they concentrated their artillery on the area. Hundreds drowned trying to swim across before the T-34s arrived.

The Russians identified the body of General Stemmermann among the bloody wreckage of his columns. He was carrying his Black Forest gun licence. Stemmermann had been killed by a shell splinter, but several SS officers shot themselves. Of his command, the Soviets claimed to have killed 55,000 and captured 18,000 (which would have meant Stemmermann's divisions were all at full establishment). There were between 50,000 and 60,000 men trapped at Cherkassy/Korsun and it is likely that less than half of them escaped. The SS Wiking and Wallonien formations retained their unit integrity and crossed the river, but the Belgians suffered 70 per cent losses in the process. Konev was promoted to Marshal of the Soviet Union and Rotmistrov (5th Guards Tank Army) became the first 'Marshal of Armoured Forces'.

LEFT *A PzKpfw V Ausf.A of unknown unit, pictured in the Russian winter of 1943–44. In December 1943 the German army had about 2,000 tanks on the eastern front, of which half were reported as operational. By early 1944 the Panzer divisions were supposed to be organised with one regiment of PzKpfw IVs and one of Panthers. (David Smith)*

BELOW *A StuG and Panzer III captured at Cherkassy. The surrounded Germans shot some of their own wounded before attempting to escape back to their own lines. (US Army)*

THE 'MUD OFFENSIVE'

Konev celebrated his promotion by resuming the offensive, despite the persisting freeze/thaw weather conditions. In what Soviet veterans would remember as the 'mud offensive' – the roads consisted of liquid mud deeper than the soldiers' boots – the 2nd Ukrainian Front drove back the German 8th Army (Hube) and liberated Uman. The advance continued to the River Bug and by March 1944, Konev's men had crossed the border into Romania. While the T-34 could slither its way across the waterlogged terrain, few German vehicles could and hundreds of tanks, half-tracks and other vehicles had to be blown up and abandoned while their crews squelched westwards on foot. Neither Konev's guns nor his supply lorries could keep up with the advance, and the leading elements were supplied by Soviet aircraft.

Zhukov took personal command of the 1st Ukrainian Front for another ambitious attempt to encircle the Germans. His intended victims – 20 or so under strength divisions of 1st Panzer Army – were cut off by the end of March after the Soviet 1st Tank Army stormed across the River Dnestr. Once again, Hitler insisted his soldiers hold their positions regardless, but Field Marshal von Manstein won a furious argument with him and permission was granted for the Army to break out. The II SS Panzer Corps mounted a vigorous relief effort and for once, Zhukov was wrong-footed. The Soviets deployed in expectation of a retreat to Romania, but the Germans drove directly west for

180 miles to the German front in Galicia. The Luftwaffe concentrated its remaining strength in the east to support the operation, delivering 200–250 tons of supplies per day over the two weeks it took 1st Panzer Army to fight its way free.

After brooding for a week or so, Hitler removed Von Manstein from command of Army Group South. Without doubt one of the best commanders of World War II, Von Manstein was compelled to sit out the rest of the war. His actions behind the front line in Russia earned him an 18-year sentence at the Nuremberg war crimes trials, but he was released in 1953 to write the best-selling *Lost Victories* and play a key role in founding the post-war West German army.

Like Guderian, the urbane and charming Manstein persuaded many British and American officers that he was a 'simple soldier', untainted by the activities of the Nazis. British historian Liddell-Hart championed both of them and

FAR RIGHT *The Wehrmacht's foreign volunteers in action, 1944–45. From left to right: 1st lieutenant, Armenian Legion; 1st lieutenant, Georgian Legion; warrant officer, Osttruppen. The Georgian Legion provided battalions for the German 1st and 4th mountain regiments. (Kevin Lyles, from* Men-at-Arms 147, Foreign Volunteers of the Wehrmacht 1941–45*)*

RIGHT *A German sniper takes aim: both sides employed snipers on the eastern front, the Russians employing a number of women soldiers in this role too. (R. Tomasi)*

BELOW *Cossacks in German service stand impassively on their mounts. They were one of the few peoples of Eastern Europe that Hitler regarded with favour, but they would pay a terrible price in 1945 for backing the losing side. (Author's collection)*

Manstein is remembered today for his brilliance as a military commander. So he was; but one of his orders, cited at his trial, reads:

'The Jewish-Bolshevist system must be exterminated … The German soldier comes as the bearer of a racial concept. [He] must appreciate the necessity for the harsh punishment of Jewry … The food situation at home makes it essential that the troops should be fed off the land, and that the largest possible stocks should be placed at the disposal of the homeland. In enemy cities, a large part of the population will have to go hungry. Nothing, out of a misplaced sense of humanity, may be given to prisoners-of-war or to the population unless they are in service of the German Wehrmacht'.[77]

Nor was this an isolated instance. When commanding the 11th Army in 1941 his orders harped on about the German soldier as the 'bearer of a racial concept', and 'an avenger of all the atrocities which have been committed against him and the German people'.[78]

Manstein's removal was the latest in a series of sackings that began with the disastrous winter of 1941–2. The three army group commanders of 1941 (Von Leeb, Von Bock and Von Rundstedt) were all removed then, although Von Rundstedt was reinstated later – only to be sacked again in 1945. General Guderian was removed at the same time, although he became Inspector-General of armoured troops in 1943. Two other highly competent officers, Generaloberst Hoth and Field Marshal von Kleist, were sacked in 1943 and 1944 respectively.

Hitler's penchant for dismissing some of his best field commanders has often attracted comment, but if he failed to appreciate their military skills, he was instinctively aware of their political potential. Might sidelining so many senior figures stimulate the German officer corps to make the sort of political intervention it had so signally avoided in the 1930s? Whereas Stalin had shot his generals to head off the (admittedly

FAR LEFT *Both sides employed captured AFVs. To mark the change of ownership, this StuG carries red stars and the popular slogan 'Death to the German Occupiers'. (Author's collection)*

LEFT *Introduced in 1943 and known as the 'hunter', the SU152 mounted a 152mm (6in) howitzer on a KV-1S hull. It was primarily designed to deal with the Tiger tank. (R. Tomasi)*

BELOW *A Zimmerit-coated StuG (right) and a Nashorn (Rhinocerous) tank destroyer (left). The latter mounted an 88mm Pak 43 on the chassis of a Panzer IV. The thinly armoured fighting compartment was open-topped and its height (2.6m/8ft 8in) presented a large target. (IWM)*

unlikely) threat of a military coup, Hitler simply bribed his potential malcontents. Field Marshal von List, commander of Army Group A in 1942, was sacked that September but, like others of his kind, seems to have received cash payments from the Nazi party until 1945. In his new role, Guderian continued to clash with Hitler over many strategic issues but still found time to spend 'months travelling around Eastern Europe looking for an estate which the government could steal for him – and he did not think the one he received was adequate'.[79]

Manstein's replacement was the acerbic Walter Model, at 53 Germany's youngest Field Marshal. His brusque manner terrified subordinates and irritated superiors and even Hitler hesitated to argue with him. Despite a period in disgrace in late 1943, he had taken over Army Group North in January 1944, restored order in a brilliant

rearguard action and won his promotion. Strangely, as no part of the country remained under German control, Army Group South was renamed Army Group North Ukraine.

On 10 April 1944 General Malinovsky, commander of the 3rd Ukrainian Front, liberated his home town of Odessa. Until a few weeks before its hurried evacuation, the city had been occupied not by the Germans, but by the Romanians. Alexander Werth visited Odessa some days after it changed hands. He was immediately struck by the large numbers of young people there – in vivid contrast to his experience of liberated Russian and Ukrainian towns where only the old and very young remained. The Romanian regime regarded Odessa as a valuable prize; its people as citizens of 'Romanian Transniestria' and not to be dragged off as slaves by the Germans.

RIGHT *The T-34/76 remained the standard Soviet tank during the battles of 1944, despite the appearance of the first new heavy tanks and the T-34/85. This T-34/E is distinguishable by the commander's raised cupola. (Author's collection)*

FAR RIGHT *Fighting in the Eastern Crimea, early 1944, on the eve of the German retreat to Sevastopol. The Crimea was important to both sides as an air base, but the German attempt to hang on to it doomed the 17th Army to disaster. (R. Tomasi)*

BELOW *One way to demolish an SU85 assault gun: the 'Goliath' was a small tracked vehicle that carried an explosive charge. It was widely used in the ferocious street battles in Warsaw in August 1944. (IWM)*

LIBERATION OF THE CRIMEA

On 11 April the Soviet 3rd Ukrainian Front (Tolbukin) broke into the Crimea from the north while a diversionary offensive crashed against the heavily-fortified Perekop isthmus. Tolbukhin's divisions fanned out to overrun the northern part of the Crimea and the German–Romanian forces in the Eastern Crimea stampeded back to Sevastopol to avoid being cut off. The German attempt to cling onto the Crimea was perhaps foolhardy, but it had many good airfields equipped for all-weather operations in range of Soviet industrial targets and the Romanian oil fields that were crucial to German fuel supplies. It was also the best place from which to fly strategic materials between Germany and Japan: in April a Junkers Ju-290 flew from Odessa to Mukden, Manchuria, with four tons of optical equipment, returning with a consignment of molybdenum. Planned missions from the Crimea were out of the question as by 16 April the German 17th Army was hemmed into Sevastopol.

Hitler ordered 'Fortress Sevastopol' to hold on until the last man; after all, the Red Army had defended it for 250 days in 1941–2. What he got was a German Dunkirk. The commander of the

LEFT *German soldiers of Army Group North snatch some time to write home. Soldiers' correspondence was closely monitored by the Nazi Party, not just to identify dissenters but to also gauge army morale.* (IWM)

BELOW *This T-34 took part in the breakthrough that ended the siege of Leningrad. T-34s lasted an average of six months from completion to destruction: only about a quarter of Soviet tank men survived the loss of their vehicle.* (R. Tomasi)

17th Army, Generaloberst Jänicke, reported the position to be untenable – and he knew an impossible situation when he saw one. He had commanded 4th Corps in the Stalingrad pocket (he was flown out and replaced by General Pfeffer before the surrender). Hitler sacked him. Evacuation began in the first days of May as the Soviets pounded the hastily-dug entrenchments. Approximately 40,000 troops were shipped away

with strangely little interference by Soviet naval forces which remained unwilling to challenge German control of the Black Sea. Although the Black Sea Fleet had a battleship, six cruisers, 21 destroyers, and 30 submarines, the threat of air attack, mines and the 16 'S'-boats and six coastal U-Boats operated there by the Kriegsmarine [80] meant that it spent most of 1942–44 inactive at Batum.

RIGHT *An MG42 machine gun team ready for action. This was the German infantry's key weapon in the defensive battles of 1944. By firing on the Soviet infantry, it separated the foot soldiers from the T-34s. However, opening fire obviously risked attracting the attention of the Soviet armour. (IWM)*

In the absence of a naval threat, the evacuation could have continued, but the perimeter collapsed on 9 May. Tolbukhin had brought forward his heavy artillery which blasted enough gaps for his infantry divisions to break in. The Germans abandoned the city and conducted a fighting withdrawal to the Hersones peninsula, seven kilometres down the coast. Some 30,000 men found themselves trapped on this tiny spit of land, no more than one kilometre across at its neck. A few thousand were rescued until Soviet artillery drove off the boats. Once the beach itself was under fire from Katyushas the game was up. On 12 May the survivors surrendered. Total German losses in the Crimea were 50,000 dead and 61,000 captured.

The return of Soviet rule to the Crimea involved more than the usual hunt for collabora-tors. Since the Crimean Tartars had co-operated with the Germans, helping to hunt down Soviet partisans and volunteering for military service, Stalin deported the entire population – 500,000 people – to central Asia/Siberia. Similar treatment had been meted out to the peoples of the North Caucasus after the German withdrawal: altogether over a million civilians were uprooted from their villages, often with no warning. Since most of the collaborators slipped away with the Germans, Soviet vengeance fell mainly on women and children. Over 100,000 NKVD troops were devoted to organising the deportations, which continued, especially in the Baltic States, until after the war. At the Party Congress in 1956 Khruschev joked that Stalin would have deported all 40 million Ukrainians too, if only he had the rail capacity and somewhere to put them.

CHAPTER NINE

PRUSSIAN ROULETTE

*'There is only one thing worse than fighting
a war with allies: and that is fighting one without them.'*

Winston Churchill

By the spring of 1944 it was obvious that the Western Allies were poised to land in France. It would be the biggest amphibious operation in history, and if it came off, Germany would lose the war. The D-Day landings were such a triumph that their success is often regarded as inevitable, and certainly by 7 June the Germans had lost their only serious opportunity to liquidate the beachheads. However, the Allied victory in Normandy was the product of many factors and was by no means assured when the spring thaw spread through Russia and Stavka began to plan its operations for the summer.

German strategy for 1944 was based on three assumptions: had they been right, history might have followed a very different course. The first was that the Allied invasion would be in the Pas de Calais. This involved the shortest sea crossing and would position the ground forces for the most direct route to the Reich. The second assumption

was that the next Soviet offensive would fall in the south, further exploiting the spectacular success of the winter offensive that had brought them to the borders of Romania and up to the Carpathians. This made political and economic sense. From here, the Soviets could strike directly into southern Poland, break into Hungary and/or push south into Romania to overrun the oil fields that sustained the German forces. The third basis for German strategy was a new-found ability to strike back at strategic targets. Where the Luftwaffe bomber force had failed, V1 and V2 ballistic missiles would succeed.

The D-Day campaign is justly celebrated for the brilliant deception plan that played on German fears; fooling them into maintaining large forces around Calais even after the Allies were ashore in Normandy. The Soviet summer offensive of 1944 – Operation Bagration – was preceded by an equally successful deception scheme that drew the bulk of the Ostheer to Army Group North

LEFT *Soviet infantry wade across a river, covered by a machine gun team. The ability of the Soviets to cross rivers using improvised methods constantly surprised the German army, as did the tenacity with which Soviet troops defended the smallest bridgehead. (Author's collection)*

RIGHT *Knights' Cross winner Sturmbannführer Kaiser uses a British Churchill tank as a desk. By early 1944 there were some 1,200 lend-lease tanks in front line service with the Red Army, although the majority were Valentines. From late 1943 M4 Shermans began to arrive in large numbers. (IWM)*

BELOW RIGHT *A Hummel self-propelled 150mm gun, based on the chassis of a Panzer IV. About 750 were built from 1943 onwards. (R. Tomasi)*

BOTTOM *Soviet soldiers examine captured German SiG33 150mm howitzers. These short-range weapons provided close support within German infantry divisions. (IWM)*

Ukraine. And even after the blow fell on 22 June, the anniversary of the German invasion three years earlier, German intelligence persisted in its belief that the major Soviet effort was still to come. The result was the greatest German defeat of the war; the annihilation of Army Group Centre. Meanwhile Hitler's last hope, that his secret weapons would turn the course of the war, was to prove equally false. The Allied air forces mounted an intensive campaign against the launch sites and missile factories, reducing the number of missile launches to a fraction of what they could have been.

There were 22 Panzer and Panzer-grenadier divisions on the Russian front in May 1944; nine in Army Group North Ukraine, nine in Army Group South Ukraine, but only three were allotted to Army Group Centre. The Ostheer had about 700 tanks and 1,000 assault guns operational,[81] Army Group Centre's armoured support consisted almost entirely of StuG assault gun batteries. The Soviet offensive, conducted by four Fronts, was spearheaded by 2,715 tanks, now

including Guard heavy tank units with IS-2s. Each of the eight tank corps had three regiments of SU-76/122/152s; a total of 1,355 assault guns took part in the attack. The assault was supported by some 24,000 guns which pulverised the thinly-held German front line with a hurricane bombardment. Above the battlefields, Soviet fighters were practically unchallenged and neither Heinkel He-111 nor Junkers Ju-88s could survive in daylight. Even Junkers Ju-188s were being intercepted at 30,000ft. The only German bombers that could get through were Heinkel He-177s, which relied on close formation flying and their heavy defensive firepower. But since fewer than 200 were completed between 1944 and 1945, their impact was only marginal.

THE DEFEAT OF ARMY GROUP CENTRE

The front collapsed within days. Vitebsk was surrounded on 24 June, Soviet forces advanced rapidly around Bobruisk, and crossed the Dnepr to by-pass the Germans in Mogilev, who were

SOVIET OFFENSIVES 1944

Soviet forces swept across the Western Ukraine, encountering resistance not just from the Germans, but from Ukrainian guerrillas, who in fact killed Marshal Vatutin. By the summer, the German Army Group Centre occupied a wide salient north of the Pripyat marshes.

Soviet deception measures fooled the Germans into expecting another assault in the south, and the stage was set for the greatest German defeat of the war.

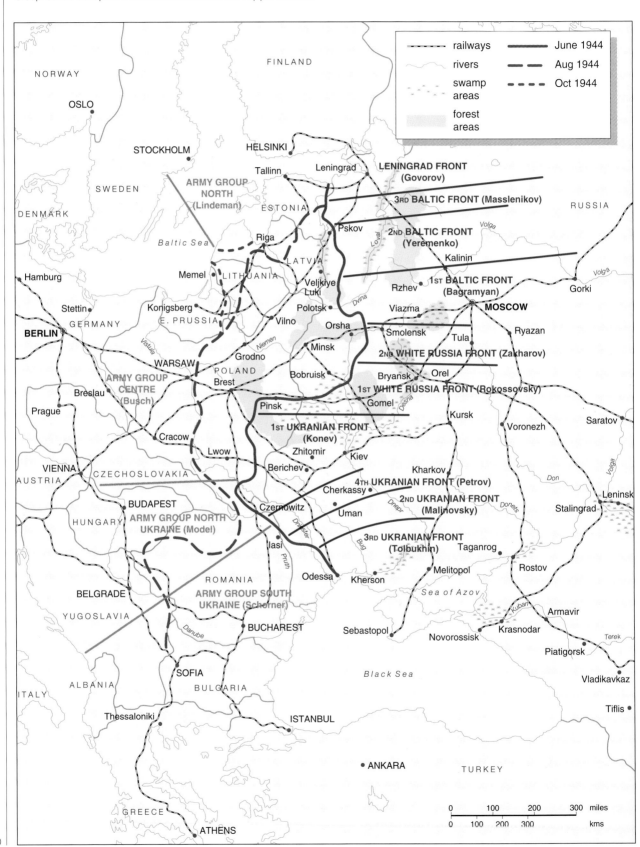

Legend:
- railways
- rivers
- swamp areas
- forest areas
- June 1944
- Aug 1944
- Oct 1944

NORWAY
OSLO
FINLAND
SWEDEN
STOCKHOLM
HELSINKI
DENMARK
Baltic Sea
Hamburg
Stettin
Memel
Riga
ESTONIA
Tallinn
Leningrad
LENINGRAD FRONT (Govorov)
3RD BALTIC FRONT (Masslenikov)
Pskov
2ND BALTIC FRONT (Yeremenko)
Volga
RUSSIA
ARMY GROUP NORTH (Lindeman)
LATVIA
Velikiye Luki
Kalinin
Volga
Gorki
Konigsberg
LITHUANIA
GERMANY
E. PRUSSIA
Polotsk
Dvina
Rzhev
1ST BALTIC FRONT (Bagramyan)
MOSCOW
Ryazan
BERLIN
Vilno
Orsha
Smolensk
Viazma
Tula
Breslau
Grodno
Niemen
Minsk
2ND WHITE RUSSIA FRONT (Zakharov)
Prague
WARSAW
POLAND
Brest
Bobruisk
Bryansk
Orel
1ST WHITE RUSSIA FRONT (Rokossovsky)
ARMY GROUP CENTRE (Busch)
Pinsk
Gomel
Desna
Kursk
Saratov
Cracow
Zhitomir
Kiev
1ST UKRANIAN FRONT (Konev)
Voronezh
Vistula
Lwow
Berichev
Kharkov
Don
Volga
VIENNA
AUSTRIA
CZECHOSLOVAKIA
4TH UKRANIAN FRONT (Petrov)
Cherkassy
2ND UKRANIAN FRONT (Malinovsky)
Leninsk
BUDAPEST
ARMY GROUP NORTH UKRAINE (Model)
Czernowitz
Uman
Dnieper
Donets
Stalingrad
HUNGARY
Dniester
Iasi
3RD UKRANIAN FRONT (Tolbukhin)
Taganrog
BELGRADE
ARMY GROUP SOUTH UKRAINE (Schorner)
Pruth
Bug
Odessa
Kherson
Melitopol
Rostov
YUGOSLAVIA
Danube
BUCHAREST
Sea of Azov
Kuban
Armavir
Krasnodar
Terek
ROMANIA
Sebastopol
Novorossisk
Piatigorsk
SOFIA
BULGARIA
Black Sea
Vladikavkaz
ITALY
ALBANIA
Tiflis
Thessaloniki
ISTANBUL
ANKARA
TURKEY
GREECE
ATHENS

| 0 | 100 | 200 | 300 | miles |
| 0 | 100 | 200 | 300 | kms |

ordered to hold their ground to the last man – as if it mattered. Within a week, the ominous gaps between major German forces showed no signs of closing. The Soviet 5th Guards Tank Army drove a wedge between the German 3rd Panzer and 4th Armies: into the gulf between the 4th Army and 9th Army plunged the Soviet 4th Guards Cavalry Corps.

Hitler's micro-management of the war in Russia had reached such ludicrous lengths that it was said officers were afraid to move a sentry from the window to the door without permission from OKH. His reaction to the disaster was entirely consistent. On 27 June, he sacked the commander of the 9th Army (who at least was able to fly to East Prussia to be dismissed, unlike his hapless soldiers). The commander of Army Group Centre, Field Marshal Busch lasted only another day before he was removed in favour of Field Marshal Model. But not even the 'fireman of the eastern front' could rescue much from the wreckage. Although German reinforcements were rushing

to stem the tide, the Soviet staff work was of a high order and their armoured forces exploited the open front with the same panache the Panzers had demonstrated in 1941. They broke through to Minsk, trapping thousands of Germans east of the city.

So many pockets were created by the disintegration of the front (and the Soviet offensive was still in full swing) that there was no prospect of relief efforts – the isolated troops were on their own. And since the local partisans had been subjected to the most savage counter-guerrilla operations earlier in the year, they seized the opportunity to take the most terrible revenge against German soldiers unlucky enough to fall into their hands. As the advancing Soviet formations discovered more than one train packed with Russian children, ready for deportation, the Red Army was not in forgiving mood either. Nevertheless, the Russians received the first mass surrenders by German units: four German corps

laid down their arms in the forests outside Minsk. Across Belorussia the Red Army took 150,000 prisoners, parading 57,000 of them through Moscow on 17 July. In five weeks, the German army had lost 300,000 men. Up to 30 divisions were removed from the German order of battle, 17 never re-formed.

The mass of German forces in Army Group North Ukraine were unable to help. On 13 July, Konev's 1st Ukrainian Front attacked into Galicia, liberating L'vov and pressing on to the River San and the old World War I fortress at Premysl. At the end of the month, the Soviet 1st, 3rd and 4th Tank Armies reached the Vistula around Sandomierz and established several bridgeheads, which were promptly subjected to furious counter-attacks. However, as the Germans had learned, Soviet bridgeheads were all but impossible to dislodge and despite intensive fighting, they failed to drive the Russians into the river.

Many people, in Russia as well as the west, had dismissed talk of concentration camps as so much propaganda. There had been innumerable atrocity stories in World War I that had subsequently proved false, and the tales of Auschwitz were widely regarded in similar light. But on 23 July 1944 the full horror of the Nazi regime was exposed by the Red Army. Not far from the Polish city of Lublin, the Germans had built the extermination camp of Majdenek. Similar establishments like Belzec, Sobibor and Treblinka

RIGHT *Soldiers of the Spanish 'Blue' division on the Leningrad front, where they fought from 1941–43. Although some volunteers stayed on, General Franco withdrew the division as it became clear that Germany would lose the war. (IWM)*

BELOW RIGHT *Holding frontages of about 30km with just six battalions, German divisions were unable to create an in-depth defence. In positions such as this, the soldiers awaited the massive artillery bombardment that signalled the start of a new Soviet offensive. (Author's collection)*

BOTTOM *German soldiers on the eastern front found themselves on battlefields that would have been horribly familiar to their fathers in 1914–18. Here, with MG42s and a Panzerfaust ready, a group of Panzergrenadiers dig in on the Iasi front, in northern Romania. (R. Tomasi)*

had already been closed and burned down after the extermination of Polish Jews was completed; Treblinka had even been turned into a farm and pine trees planted to hide the evidence.

There had not been time to do the same at Majdenek. All the machinery was there – concrete gas chambers labelled *Bad und Desinfektion*, the crematorium capable of burning 2,000 bodies a day, a barn containing 850,000 pairs of shoes and a fresh mass-grave where the remaining prisoners were shot and buried as the SS departed. The Soviet newspaper *Pravda* printed a full account which confirmed the revelations of escaped prisoners-of-war who had been swept back into the Russian army as it approached the German border. 'It was with a whiff of Majdenek in their nostrils that thousands of Russian soldiers were to fight their way into East Prussia', noted Alexander Werth[82] whose own report on the death camp was spiked by the BBC. The War in the East had been merciless enough since 1941, and as the Soviet forces prepared to invade Germany, the opportunity to take vengeance was openly anticipated.

Ehrenburg's rabid propaganda continued to stoke the fires of hatred well into 1945.

On 20 July Hitler survived the penultimate of the nine assassination attempts made against him between 1933 and 1945. It was the most-nearly successful too – a bomb exploding under the conference table at his headquarters in East Prussia. Failing to check he was dead, the plotters attempted to seize power but their networks in Berlin, Vienna and Paris were rounded up as a vengeful Führer co-ordinated the machinery of state by telephone from Rastenburg.

Even the most well-adjusted individual might have become to believe that he benefited from divine intervention, if spared from death on so many occasions. In Hitler's case, this latest manifestation of *Fortuna* reinforced all of his most odious sentiments, which had immediate impact on the War in the East. Proclaiming he now knew why Stalin had Tukachevsky shot, Hitler appointed Nazi political officers to all military headquarters. Martin Bormann and Heinrich Himmler became regular attendants at the

Führer's daily military conferences. Discipline in the German army became completely dislocated from the pre-war legal system. 'Flying military courts', a dreadful mixture of Gestapo officials, military police, SS, and SD men, arbitrarily executed soldiers and civilians alike. Kurt Zeitzler was replaced as chief-of-staff at OKH by the officer whose vigorous action against the coup attempt had restored order in Berlin – Generaloberst Heinz Guderian.

Meanwhile, the Soviet advance continued

across Poland and was approaching Warsaw. At the hub of their road and rail communications and a key crossing of the Vistula, the city was strategically vital to the Germans and they counter-attacked aggressively from 30 July. Newly-arrived in the east, and with a full regiment of Panzer IVs and a battalion of Jagdpanzer IVs, the Hermann Göring Division attacked alongside 4th Panzer Division and SS Wiking Divisions, both from Army Group North Ukraine. They drove back the Soviet 3rd Tank Corps and 8th Guards Tank Corps some 15km north-east of Warsaw. The Soviet forces had fought their way across 700km in little over a month and were reaching the culminating point of their offensive. But from 1 August, political calculation combined with military necessity to slow the Russian advance. The Polish Home Army had risen in Warsaw.

THE WARSAW RISING

The Soviet regime had been waging war on the Poles for longer than it had fought the Germans. The decision to murder the 15,000 Polish officers had been taken in 1940, over a year before the German invasion of the USSR. During the 18 months of Soviet rule in Eastern Poland, over a million Poles were deported to the GULAG. Nevertheless, by the summer of 1944 the Soviet forces included two Polish armies with a strength of some 90,000 men, such was the impact of the Nazis in their home country. The Polish people were regarded as no more than a slave labour force, and it is significant that Poland was about the only country in Eastern Europe to provide no volunteer units for the Wehrmacht or Waffen-SS. Some six million Poles, half of them Jewish, were put to death by the Germans, giving Poland the highest proportionate casualties of any nation in World War II.

Warsaw had already been the scene of one uprising: the Jews in the ghetto had fought to the death rather than be deported to the extermination camps, holding off SD and SS units for several days in April 1943 with little but pistols and petrol bombs. In August 1944 the Polish Home Army had something like 40,000 men and women under its command, loyal to the government-in-exile in London. Although only ten per cent had weapons, the decision was taken to seize control of Poland's capital before the Red Army did so. Unfortunately for the Poles, they failed to secure any of the bridges over the Vistula and during the next few weeks, the sudden passivity of the Soviet army enabled the Germans to assemble enough

LEFT *Members of the Red Army Cossack Cavalry. From left to right: captain, Kuban Cossacks; officer, Kuban Cossacks; lieutenant, Terek Cossacks. At the beginning of the war there were 13 cavalry divisions in the Red Army, the cavalry force expanding to 82 divisions by the end of 1942, although most were only brigade-size units. In mud, snow, swamps and forests, the cavalry often proved more mobile than mechanised formations. (Ron Volstad, from Men-at-Arms 216,* The Red Army of the Great Patriotic War 1941–45)

BELOW LEFT *Soviet troops taking part in Operation Bagration. From left to right: sergeant, Red Army Traffic Control; Red Army sniper; Red Army scout. By 1945 about ten per cent of the Red Army's strength consisted of women soldiers, mainly Russians. Most were medics or signallers, but some famously served as pilots, snipers or tank crew. (Ron Volstad, from Men-at-Arms 216,* The Red Army of the Great Patriotic War 1941–45)

TOP RIGHT *A PzKpfw V Ausf. G of 5.SS-Pz.-Div. 'Wiking' in action in Poland, 1944. (David Smith)*

BELOW RIGHT *A PzKpfw V Ausf. A of 5.SS-Pz.-Div. 'Wiking' pictured in action in Poland, 1944. Photographed at the same time, this Panther belongs to a different company than the one above, but has a quite different camouflage scheme. Wiking spearheaded the German counter-attacks north-east of Warsaw that stopped the Soviet advance on the Polish capital, just as the Home Army launched its ill-fated uprising. (David Smith)*

BOTTOM *Three details of a Tiger B (Henschel turret), in action 1944–45. The magnificent Tiger II could only be taken on by the heaviest Soviet AFVs, the IS-II and ISU-152. It was a superbly engineered combat vehicle, but only built in tiny quantities by comparison with Soviet or American production totals. (David Smith)*

forces to counter-attack. Hitler demanded the city be destroyed altogether, and the German units that he sent there included the most infamous in his army, including the Dirlewanger Brigade (an SS penal unit commanded by a convicted paedophile, Dr Oskar Dirlewanger)[83] and the Russian Kaminski's private army (see Chapter 6). Few barbarities known to man were absent in the slaughter that followed.

Some Soviet units – including Polish divisions under Soviet command – crossed the Vistula and entered the eastern outskirts of Warsaw in mid-September, but were unable to break through to the insurgent Home Army before German counter-attacks drove them back across the river. No doubt the front line troops, Russians as well as Poles were fighting as hard as they could, but the Germans had deployed major new armoured formations in the east. Stalin refused to allow US aircraft to use Soviet airfields when they tried to parachute supplies to the Polish resistance. 'Power-seeking criminals' was Stalin's description of the Home Army; and it suited the Soviets perfectly for the Germans to finish off what the NKVD had started in the killing fields of Katyn.

The Home Army surrendered on 2 October and to medieval cruelty, Hitler added his own brand of vindictiveness. Warsaw was systematically destroyed, buildings blown up block by block so that when the city was finally abandoned to the Russians in January 1945 little more than black-ened rubble remained.

Germany's defeats in both east and west led Heinrich Himmler to drop his racial objections to

the use of Russian soldiers. Soviet General Andrei Vlasov, an insanely ambitious officer who had championed the German cause since his capture in 1942, was wheeled out to take command of a new Russian army. Himmler promised him ten divisions. The scheme was part of the Reichsführer's expanding state-within-a-state. The Waffen-SS already included many units recruited in Eastern Europe. By the end of the year he would snatch both Cossack divisions raised by the German army, and then employed on anti-partisan operations in the Balkans – they would be retitled 15th SS Cavalry Corps.

HITLER'S ALLIES DEPART

The decisive defeat of German forces in the east, and the presence of Allied forces in France and halfway up the Italian peninsula suggested that the end of the war was only a matter of time. Italy had already changed sides, General Franco had with-drawn the Azul Spanish division and Hitler's remaining allies moved quickly to finish on the winning side too.

On 20 August, the 2nd Ukrainian Front (Malinovsky) and 3rd Ukrainian Front (Tolbukhin) launched an operation intended to conquer Romania. The Soviet forces had 92 infantry divisions between them and six tank/mechanised corps, a total of over a million men. Malinovsky attacked north-west of Iasi and established bridgeheads over the River Prut, threatening to cut off the German 6th and 8th

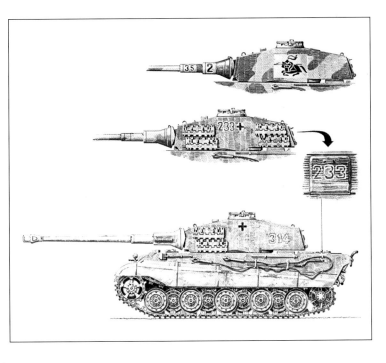

135

armies. The 3rd Ukrainian Front already had a foothold on the west bank of the Dnestr near Tiraspol, but fierce German resistance checked the assault until the Romanians followed the Italian example. On 23 August Marshal Antonescu was arrested on the orders of King Mihai. Romanian units surrendered en masse to the Soviets and within weeks they were fighting against the Germans. The German 6th Army was annihilated for a second time in the war, after its fighting retreat from Chisenau was blocked by the Soviets at the River Siret. In just ten days, Army Group South (re-named Army Group South Ukraine on 1 September) had shrunk from 500,000 Germans and 400,000 Romanians to just 200,000 Germans.

Bulgaria had been allied to Germany since 1941 and had declared war on Britain and America that December, but Hitler failed to compel King Boris to join the war against Russia, and possibly had the unfortunate monarch murdered in August 1943.[84] On 5 September 1944 Bulgaria severed diplomatic relations with

Germany, but it was not enough: the Soviet army poured across the frontier. Elements of the Bulgarian army served under Soviet command in the subsequent fighting in Hungary, while a pro-Soviet political structure was put in place. King Boris' brother, the regent Prince Cyril, was shot by the NKVD in February 1945.

Two days after Romania's defection, Finland concluded an agreement with the Soviets and the German forces there withdrew to Norway in October after the Soviet Karelian Front attacked and captured Petsamo.

Germany's last significant ally was Hungary and the regent Admiral Miklos Horthy was already having secret talks with Stalin, his representatives arriving in Moscow on 1 October 1944. An armistice was signed ten days later, but German forces in Budapest carried out a coup before it could take effect. Horthy was despatched to a concentration camp and a fanatical pro-Nazi called Ferenc Szalasi took his place. Adolf Eichmann was able to supervise the last great round-up of Jews – 437,000 people were shipped

straight to Auschwitz. The Hungarian army was reorganised under direct German control, with new formations recruited directly by the Wehrmacht. The SS began recruitment for four Hungarian SS divisions too, but these embryonic units were caught up in the retreat that began in October as the Soviet 3rd Ukrainian Front forced the Carpathian passes (with the Romanian 1st and 4th armies now part of his command). Only the arrival of substantial German reinforcements including 3rd Panzer Corps prevented the Soviets attacking Budapest itself in early November. In the teeth of repeated German counter-attacks led by 4th SS Panzer Corps, Malinovsky nevertheless succeeded in encircling the Hungarian capital at the end of December. The 8th SS Cavalry

LEFT *Soviet Cossacks celebrate their arrival in the foothills of the Carpathians. (Author's collection)*

Division Florian Geyer, the 13th Panzer Division, SS Feldherrnhalle division and several Hungarian divisions were trapped. On the other side of the lines, the former commander of the Hungarian 1st Army, General Miklos, emerged as head of a pro-Soviet provisional government, ready to be installed as soon as the Red Army could complete its conquest.

Army Group North was not destroyed in the same way as Army Groups Centre and South, but its likely fate was evident at the end of July when a Soviet offensive broke through to the Gulf of Riga. Army Group North was cut off. In mid-August the German 3rd Panzer Army managed to cut through to re-establish a slim corridor, and Army Group North fell back on Riga, but on 5 October the reorganised Soviets mounted a far greater effort using the 50 divisions of 1st and 2nd Baltic Fronts. Breaking through either side of Memel (Klaipeda) where the German 28th Corps

found itself trapped, the Soviets reached the coast in overwhelming strength. Army Group North was marooned at the end of the Kurland peninsula from Libau (Liapâja) on the Baltic to the Gulf of Riga around Tukums, a front of about 160km.

By the end of 1944 Germany had been defeated in France, with the loss of 400,000 men, and crushed in Eastern Europe with the loss of 900,000 men. The Allied armies were poised to dismember the 'thousand year Reich', and German military deployments were almost calculated to help. Hitler refused to evacuate Army Group North while his navy could still operate with relative impunity in the Baltic, major forces were retained in Norway, and the fighting in Hungary drew off what remained of Germany's armoured reserves after the lunatic adventure known to history as the Battle of the Bulge, Hitler's quixotic attempt to repeat the victory of 1940 across the same ground in December 1944.

CHAPTER TEN

GOODBYE TO BERLIN

'The hour of revenge has struck!'

Ilya Ehrenburg

Six months after the Ostheer was so badly wrong-footed and Army Group Centre driven from Belorussia to Warsaw, Generaloberst Heinz Guderian realised Hitler was poised to repeat the error. For what he described as 'political reasons', Hitler was diverting German reserves to Hungary, for a counter-attack to relieve Budapest. Guderian highlighted the obvious danger that the Soviets would attack straight across Poland and into Germany. He cited Colonel Gehlen's analysis that the Russian assault would begin on 12 January with an 11:1 superiority in infantry, 7:1 in tanks and 20:1 in artillery. Hitler told him to fire his intelligence chief, to which Guderian retorted he may as well fire his Chief-of-Staff too.

Hitler kept them both, for the time being, but Army Group Centre was not spared. On the very day Guderian had predicted, five Soviet Fronts attacked in what became known as the 'Vistula-Oder' operation. A 35km hole was torn in the German front, expanded and deepened while isolated pockets of resistance were reduced by follow-on forces. Warsaw was encircled, then stormed on 17 January by the 1st Polish Army: Krakow fell the next day. German units assembling for a counter-attack at Lodz were caught deploying, and swept back to the River Oder. Two of the Soviet Fronts stormed into East Prussia, pinning the 3rd Panzer Army into Königsberg

(Kaliningrad) and the Samland peninsula. The beleaguered Germans were joined by the former garrison of Memel, evacuated on 29 January under the guns of the surviving units of the German navy, including the heavy cruiser *Prinz Eugen*. The 'pocket battleships' *Lutzow* and *Scheer* bombarded the Soviet lines too, before withdrawing to Kiel and Gotenhafen. From the Baltic to Southern Poland, improvised Kampfgruppen fought desperately, firstly to win time for German forces to make good their escape, and then to break free themselves. In a fortnight, the Soviet army had advanced 400km and was poised to invade the German heartland. From their bridgeheads on the Oder to Berlin was but an hour's drive along the autobahn.

As the Soviet forces raced across Poland, the siege of Budapest continued. The last attempt to break through to the city had narrowly failed on 1 January, the trapped garrison attacking westwards to link up with a final effort by 4th SS Panzer Corps. Only about 20km separated the German and Hungarian forces, but the Soviets were able to stop them there. Throughout the rest of the month, Soviet troops fought their way into the Hungarian capital house-by-house, street-by-street, grinding their way to the Danube at incredible cost. With the bridges down and the river at their backs, the defenders were split into several pockets which finally surrendered on 18

RIGHT *A Soviet La-7 'White 27' of 176.Gv.IAP, 302 IAD, 8IAK, which saw extensive action over Germany in spring 1945. Russian aircraft dominated the sky above the battlefields, but even in the last months of the war, German forces on the eastern front could manoeuvre freely behind the frontline. In the west, the least movement in daytime tended to be punished by an Allied airstrike. (John Weal, from Aircraft of the Aces 15, Soviet Aces of World War II)*

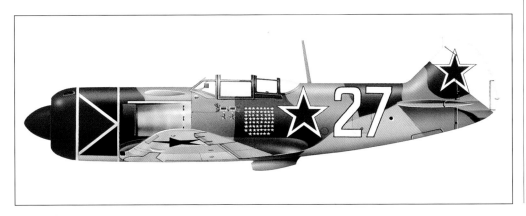

January. The same horrific process then began on the opposite bank as Buda was systematically conquered with the same combination of flame-throwers, demolition charges and point-blank fire from 8-in howitzers. With the end in sight, some 16,000 German and Hungarian troops tried to break out on 16 February but were wiped out in a series of running battles.

The last German offensive of World War II began on 6 March along the shores of Lake Balaton, Hungary. A total of 31 divisions including 11 Panzer and Panzer-grenadier divisions with up to 800 tanks took part, although many formations were at much reduced strength. The 6th SS Panzer Army which spearheaded the advance was commanded by SS Oberstgruppenführer 'Sepp' Dietrich. To preserve security, reconnaissance of the ground had been minimal and yet the early thaw had left the low-lying countryside heavily water-logged. He recognised the impossibility of his orders in the first hours. His 60-ton Tiger II heavy tanks sank up to their turrets when they tried to move off the road. Fifteen of these precious vehicles had to be abandoned. As one SS Obersturmbannführer had already signalled him when ordered to attack: ' I have tanks, not submarines. You can kiss my arse but I won't do it.' [85]

For a few days it seemed as if the old magic still worked. The Germans broke into the Soviet defences (prompting even the phlegmatic Tolbukhin to request assistance from 9th Guards Army) then prepared for the next offensive. But the German attack faced impossible odds and sputtered out in the swamp. Leaving hundreds of new tanks immobilised in the mud, the 6th Panzer Army fell back towards Vienna.

The appearance of the Soviet army on German soil prompted a mass exodus, and in some cases, mass suicide. Refugees poured westwards as the embattled German army fought for time.

LEFT *SS men take a smoke-break. By 1945 the Waffen-SS had grown to nearly a million men and drew the lion's share of new equipment. (IWM)*

BELOW *A German machine gun team moves into action. In infantry, the Ostheer was outnumbered by more than 3:1 after major forces were withdrawn to the west for the ill-fated December 1944 Ardennes offensive. (Author's collection)*

RIGHT A Jagdpanzer IV seen in East Prussia in January 1945: the lowness of its side profile is clear. Note the Panzerfaust anti-tank rockets carried by the infantry. (IWM)

For years the Nazi propaganda machine had painted the most blood-curdling images of what the 'Jewish–Bolshevik hordes' would do if they broke into the Reich. And from the moment it crossed the frontier, the Red Army's appetite for destruction and, above all, rape was practically insatiable. H.G. Wells once observed that if you push even the most civilised man far enough, you will be confronted by the hot red eyes of the caveman. The Soviets had won a war using every tool of twentieth-century industrial civilisation, yet marked their victory in the most bestial, primitive fashion. In village after village, town after town, Soviet soldiers burst into rooms of terrified civilians waving machine guns and bellowing, 'Frau Komm!' Such was the scale of horror that after the fighting was over, the Roman Catholic bishop of Berlin gave Catholic doctors permission to perform abortions. Not for the first time in the War in the East, army officers condoned their men's savagery – some exhorted them to do their worst. For Colonel-general Pavel Rybalko, commander of 3rd Guards Tank Army, it was personal – the Germans had abducted his daughter.

Among the most eager for vengeance were the slave labourers and released prisoners-of-war, who were pressed into service with Soviet divisions as the front line rolled forwards. One moment they were at the mercy of the Germans, to be starved or killed at their whim. An instant later, the roles were reversed, they were back in the Red Army, rifle in hand. Some even carried out their own imitation of the selection at the concentration camps, wading into columns of refugees to pick out all the children, which they then machine-gunned in front of their distraught parents.[86]

Between January and May 1945 some five million German civilians fled their homes. Two million were evacuated by sea from German-held ports along the Baltic, an epic amphibious rescue mission that involved the worst maritime disaster in history, the sinking of the *Wilhelm Gustoff* by the Soviet submarine *S13*. The 25,000-ton liner had over 8,000 people aboard when she sank within sight of the cruiser *Admiral Hipper* and the torpedo boat *T36*. The warships themselves already had 1,700 refugees embarked and the cruiser steamed off to avoid another torpedo. Only about 650 people survived.

Such was the power of the SS by 1945 that German civilians were left to face the Russians, while the SS commandeered shipping to empty those concentration camps near the coast. Stuffhof, near Danzig, was evacuated as the Soviets approached although about half its 4,500 remaining inmates were murdered in the process, many driven into the sea and shot.

A total of 1.39 million German civilians remain unaccounted for in the wake of 1945. If some reached safety but never advertised it, many more people died lonely deaths not included in the cold statistics of World War II. Unknown numbers of Allied prisoners-of-war, slave labourers from Poland or the Balkans – and even the USSR – were all subjected to the dreadful vengeance of the Red Army.

The Soviet leadership tried to rein in its soldiers as early as February, a *Red Star* editorial proclaiming that just because the Germans 'publicly raped our women, it does not mean we must do the same.' Ehrenburg's rabid cries for revenge were explicitly criticised in *Pravda* which proclaimed the obvious truth that 'it is unwise and un-Marxist to think all Germans were Nazis, to be treated only as subhumans.' Stalin was more concerned that his soldiers were destroying all sorts of facilities that would be useful for rebuilding the USSR's shattered economy after the war.

THE FINAL BATTLE

The German army had fewer than two million troops left on the eastern front by spring 1945. Of these, up to three-quarters of a million were trapped in various ports like the fortress of Königsberg, and in Army Group North (now Army Group Kurland) on its remote and irrelevant Baltic peninsula. The Red Army was over six million strong, and its objective was Berlin.

By March 1945 British and American armies had reached the Elbe, 120km from the German capital. The Russians were much closer, about 60km east of Berlin, and Stalin was determined that his forces would take the city. It had not gone unnoticed that the Germans were surrendering in large numbers in the west, while the Ostheer fought with incredible tenacity to keep the Russians at bay. Throughout 1942–43, the British and Americans had held back from fighting in mainland Europe, while the Red Army took on the main body of the German army. The Soviet leadership remained convinced that this was a deliberate, cynical policy.

Zhukov's 1st Belorussian Front consisted of nine armies, including two tank armies, formed up directly east of the city along the River Oder. Konev's 1st Ukrainian Front was to the south and comprised eight armies, two of which were tank armies. Closed up to the River Neisse, Konev's forces had the River Spree to cross before they could sweep up to Berlin.

ENDGAME 1945

By the beginning of 1945 the Soviet army was poised to conquer Germany. Hitler withdrew to a hastily-prepared bunker in Berlin, still preaching victory. His generals began to ignore his orders, trying to hold back the Soviets at the cost of allowing the Western Allies to overrun western Germany. By April the game was up and many German units broke contact with the Soviets to flee westwards in the hope of surrendering to the British or Americans.

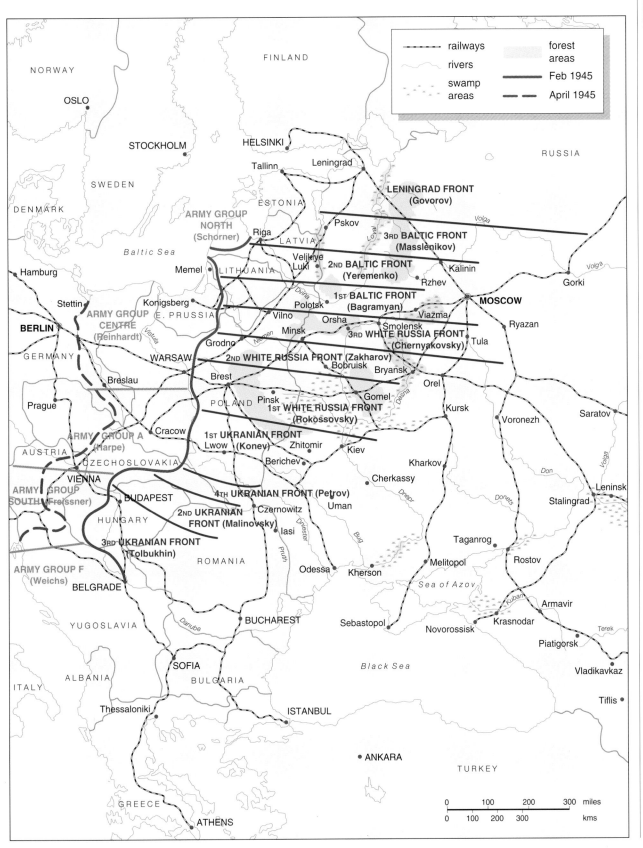

As preparations for the final Soviet offensive began, the fighting continued without a break along the Baltic shores and in Austria. Unlike many cities declared a 'fortress' by Hitler, Königsberg had some modern concrete defences which were augmented by every defensive measure German engineers could devise. With the

sea at their backs, and evacuation impossible under such constant air attack, the German garrison held each position with the same cold courage as the defenders of Sevastopol had displayed three years earlier. When the casemates were blown in by heavy artillery and the defensive guns beaten into silence, the Russian storming parties swarmed into the trenches and tunnels; but there were always handfuls of survivors fighting on with sub-machine guns and grenades. Despite the fearful odds, they continued to counter-attack, disputing every yard until 9 April when the Soviets broke into the middle of the city. General Lasch and 92,000 German soldiers surrendered: 42,000 troops lay dead in the ruins, along with an estimated 25,000 civilians – a quarter of the city's population. As Königsberg's agony ended, an equally ferocious battle was taking place in Vienna, where the defenders had to be prised out of every building, and a cadre of SS troops put up the most incredible resistance around the remaining Danube bridges. An attempted coup by communist sympathisers failed, but it enabled elements of 5th Guards Tank Corps to penetrate the defences, and the city fell on 13 April.

The Soviet attack on Berlin involved over two million men and women, 6,000 tanks and self-propelled guns and some 40,000 guns, mortars and rocket-launchers. Their route was barred by between 750,000 and a million German troops,

with about 500 tanks and 1,000 assault guns. Zhukov opened his part of the offensive with an artillery barrage that would have impressed veterans of 1917–18: with up to 295 guns per 1,000m of front, his gunners would fire 7.1 million rounds of ammunition.

The German forces were under the command of Army Group Vistula, initially commanded by the head of the SS, Heinrich Himmler, whose empire had grown in inverse proportion to that of his master. Guderian shrewdly persuaded Himmler to lay down this particular burden: the defence would be masterminded by General-oberst Gotthard Heinrici, for two years the commander of the 4th Army on the Moscow front. The latter's first task was an impossible counter-attack at Küstrin, demanded by the Führer, which began with great courage and ended in heavy casualties but without breaking through. Hitler sacked Guderian for the second and final time after he passionately defended the officers and men committed to this futile enterprise.

It may have been at this time that Heinrici and other senior commanders like Busse and Wenck (commanding the 9th and 12th Armies respectively) accepted that the war was over. Hitler was doomed, and all that mattered now was to save as many of their men and German civilians from the Soviets. Hitler's previously sensitive political antennae failed to detect this hidden agenda, even when Heinrici's forces conspicuously failed to protect Berlin, preferring instead to keep escape

routes open either side of the city while his men facing the Western Allies were shuttled east to prolong resistance as long as possible. The Führer's devoted generals Keitel and Jodl scented treachery, but when Keitel visited Heinrici to remonstrate, he was met with drawn weapons by Heinrici and Manteuffel's staff officers.

Konev's troops stormed the River Neisse on 16 April: 60-ton bridges were in position that afternoon and his tanks were ready to exploit all the way to the Spree. Zhukov's attack faltered, the staggering intensity of his artillery barrage notwithstanding. On the Seelow heights, enough German defenders emerged from their bunkers to cut down the Soviet infantry, in spite of (or possibly because of) a line of searchlights shining in their faces as the attack went in. Zhukov allowed impatience to overcome his military judgement, and ordered both his tank armies (six corps including 1,337 tanks/assault guns) to attack without waiting for the infantry to break into the defences.

He could override both the battle plan and his furious infantry commanders, but Zhukov could not command the Germans to give in. Carefully-concealed anti-tank guns and a few surviving tank destroyers commenced a frightful slaughter of the Soviet armour as the vehicles struggled across the swampy plain below. When the tanks fought their way on to the German position, they found them-selves among minefields and were attacked by infantry teams with Panzerfausts. Smarting after an angry telephone exchange with Stalin in Moscow,

heading north where Rybalko's 3rd Guards Tank Army met Katukov's 1st Guards Tank Army, part of Zhukov's Front, trapping the remains of the German 9th Army between them.

At the daily briefings in the Berlin bunker to which Hitler had withdrawn in mid-January, Generaloberst Hans Krebs, Guderian's replacement as OKW Chief-of-Staff, brought a welcome professional calm to the proceedings. No defeatism, no hysterical demands for reinforcements or complaints about attempting the impossible. Albert Speer realised it was a cunning game. The Führer ordered this or that division to fall back on Berlin, others to hold on to 'fortresses' from Czechoslovakia to Pomerania, and Krebs played along with the fantasy. Just as Speer raced around the collapsing Reich countermanding Hitler's vindictive demolition orders, so Krebs kept Hitler busy manoeuvring phantom armies across the briefing maps. It diverted Hitler from issuing more lunatic orders that the SS were still all too ready to insist were obeyed. Field Marshal Kesselring played along too: during his last visit to the bunker he committed his forces in

LEFT *A 1945 SA-Mann, Wehrmannschaft, in Styria. The SA had lost its* raison d'être *once Hitler achieved power. Elements of the SA fought with the improvised Volksturm formations in 1945. (Ron Volstad, from* Men-at-Arms 220, The SA 1921–45: Hitler's Stormtroopers)

BELOW *An SU-57 (T48 57mm GMC) of the Soviet Independent TD Brigade. The Red Army seldom repainted its American vehicles, many retaining not just the olive drab scheme but the Allied white star too. (Steven Zaloga)*

BOTTOM *An M4A2 (76mm)W of the Soviet 9th Guards Tank Brigade, 1st Guards Mechanised Corps. The USA supplied 2,007 M4 Shermans with 75mm guns and 2,095 M4s with the 76mm weapon. (Steven Zaloga)*

Zhukov piled in extra tanks as the battle continued into the night. Still suspicious that the Western Allies might drive on Berlin – Eisenhower's willingness to give the Soviets a free run at the city seemed too naive to be true – Stalin chose this moment to stoke the notorious rivalry between Marshals Zhukov and Konev. He removed the agreed Front boundaries just in front of Berlin: whoever advanced the fastest would have the honour of storming the Nazi capital.

Zhukov's men stormed the Seelow heights the next day, after 800 aircraft bombed the defences and the gunners released another formidable concentration of fire. However, Konev's tanks had not only reached the River Spree, but a T-34 had taken the plunge and driven straight into the river where the map marked a ford. Under fire all the way, it roared across, the water surging around its hull until it clattered up the opposite bank, firing its machine-guns. Exploitation continued, with Konev's armour

RIGHT *An IS-2M of the Polish 4th Ind. Heavy Tank Regiment, in action in Germany 1945. The white recognition stripes were painted on Soviet AFVs in early 1945 to identify them to the forces of the Western Allies. (Steven Zaloga)*

the west to a massive counter-attack, with not the least intention of carrying it out.

Hitler was 56 years old on 20 April. There was a brief party held in the Chancellery before a gloomy military briefing in the bunker. It was the last time he would see his leading henchmen Göring and Himmler. Before he vanished underground again, cameras recorded Hitler's last public appearance, shambling along, distributing medals to 20 teenage boys from the Hitlerjugend. Below with his generals, Hitler committed himself to dying in Berlin, disappointing those in his diminishing entourage that were egging him on to fly to Bavaria.

On 21 April the Soviet 3rd Guards Tank Army stormed Zossen, just 15 miles south of Berlin. This leafy hamlet was nothing less than the brain of the Wehrmacht. Forty feet underground, its entrances hidden among the trees and scattered buildings, lay a labyrinth of tunnels, conference rooms and the largest telephone exchange in Europe – 'Central 500', code-named 'Zeppelin'. In continuous operation since 1939 and connected to every major German headquarters, it was to here that Hitler had been urged to retreat, not the incomplete shelter beneath the Berlin Chancellery. While the Nazi leaders gathered for Hitler's last party, German officers were grabbing their paperwork and piling everything moveable on to lorries bound for Berlin. The evacuation was carried out in such a hurry that when Rybalko's men broke

into the complex they found telephones still ringing and teleprinters churning out signals.

On 22 April Hitler finally blurted out the obvious – the war was lost. The same day, the bunker echoed with the incongruous sound of youthful laughter as Magda Goebbels shepherded her six children inside. She carried a small case with just one spare dress; the children were allowed one toy each. By 24 April the last roads out of Berlin were cut and, just a day later, the Soviets overran Templehof airport. Communications between the capital and the remainder of the Reich were precarious. Hanna Reitsch flew into the city using the Unter den Linden as a runway, leaving by Arado Ar 96 from the Brandenburg Gate. In its last aerial resupply missions of the war, the Luftwaffe delivered crates of anti-tank shells from Junkers Ju-52s, putting down on the road after Speer's giant lamp posts were removed. Hitler's own pilot Hans Baur still had several long range aircraft at Gatow, the last airfield in German hands, including a Junkers Ju-390 with enough fuel to reach Manchuria. But the perimeter was steadily shrinking and Soviet soldiers were on the edge of the Tiergarten, just 3,000m from the bunker.

The atmosphere in the Berlin bunker was doom-laden, claustrophobic and poisonous. Treachery was in the air. Hitler eventually commanded the arrest of both Göring and Himmler for secretly trying to negotiate their

LEFT *The formidable Tiger II was a match for any Allied tank, but only 353 were built in 1944 and 112 in 1945. The total production run was less than half the monthly output of the Soviet factory at Chelyabinsk (Tankograd). (US National Archive)*

CENTRE *A knocked-out T-34 surrounded by corpses. The German army continued to fight with cold professionalism, inflicting heavy losses on the attacking Soviet forces. (Author's collection)*

BOTTOM *The Cossacks serving with the German army were employed against the Yugoslav partisans in 1944–45 and managed to surrender to the British at the end of the war. Horrific scenes followed the British government's decision to hand them and their families over to the Soviet government. (IWM)*

own peace deals with the Allies. Himmler's representative in Berlin, the cavalry general SS Gruppenführer Hermann Fegelein, was shot outside the bunker on the orders of Gestapo chief Müller. Nothing, not even his marriage to Eva Braun's sister, could save him after the revelation of Himmler's faithlessness – although the exposure of his mistress as a British secret agent did not help his case.[87]

The army defending Berlin was an odd mixture of teenage conscripts (some little more than children), old men recruited into the Volksturm, and hard-bitten army veterans like the men of 9th Parachute and 18th Panzer-grenadier divisions. There were many non-Germans too, many evacuated from Kurland via Danzig to make their final stand. The 11th SS Panzer-grenadier Division Nordland was originally a regiment in the SS Wiking Division. In 1943 it had been expanded to divisional size, with a regiment of Danes and one of Norwegians. The 23rd SS Panzer-grenadier Division Nederland consisted of Dutch volunteers. The 15th SS Waffen-grenadier division Lettische Nr.1 was recruited in Latvia and its soldiers now had no home to return to.

These units were joined in Berlin by one foreign company that had to fight its way into the city from the west. Assembled from the surviving members of the French SS Division Charlemagne after its disbandment, this fanatical band included a tank killer team that had all won the Iron Cross 1st class.

Both leading Soviet commanders were in at the kill. Although the battle for the Seelow heights cost his men excessive losses, Zhukov pushed on to assault the city from the north and east, while Konev's men attacked from the south. Zhukov's post-war attempts to claim sole credit seems not just petty but irrelevant – Konev's front line was within 200m of the Reichstag when the fighting ceased. The German defenders included some of the most lethal professional soldiers the world has ever seen. What some of the others lacked in military skills, they made up for with the courage of despair. So although the perimeter steadily shrank, each room, each storey, each city block cost the Soviets dearly. Since ancient times the storming of a city that refuses to surrender has been accompanied by gruesome acts of brutality. In Berlin the fearful casualties suffered by many Russian units were enough to trigger savage retaliation when opportunity presented itself. And, as the capital of the Nazi regime, Berlin was the obvious target for Soviet vengeance. The carnage that followed led to uncounted deaths – the city's population was already swollen with refugees when Soviet tanks blocked the last escape routes.

At 6.00 a.m. on Monday 30 April the commander of the Chancellery area defences – the citadel – was woken by a telephone call from the Bunker. SS Brigadeführer (Brigadier-general) Wilhelm Mohnke was just 34 years old. He had risen rapidly through the ranks of 1st SS Panzer Division Leibstandarte and had commanded the division during the Ardennes offensive. Now he was summoned to keep his promise to Hitler. As the Soviet grip on the city had tightened, Hitler had asked Mohnke to report when, in his professional judgement, the enemy was within 24 hours of breaking into the bunker. Since the Russians had captured the Tiergarten and even penetrated the subway under the Friederichstrasse, Mohnke had no choice but to tell Hitler it was finished. The SS general was treated to a Hitler monologue that could have come straight from the pages of Mein Kampf.[88] Armed with a copy of Hitler's will and testament, Mohnke returned to his headquarters to conduct a last ditch defence. Hitler and his new bride committed suicide that afternoon.

Mohnke returned to the Bunker the following evening, shortly after Magda Goebbels systematically murdered her sleeping children with cyanide capsules. Then he watched Joseph and Magda Goebbels walk upstairs to the courtyard where they committed suicide. General Krebs, who spoke fluent Russian, had already opened negotiations, coming face to face with none other than General Chuikov, defender of Stalingrad.

LEFT *IS-II heavy tanks take part in a Soviet victory parade in 1945. Hitler's war against the USSR had led to the destruction of his regime, and the deaths of about 30 million people. (IWM)*

Brigadeführer Mohnke found himself leading one of the break-out groups, side-lining the odious Martin Bormann who was now just another refugee. In teams, in ones and twos, the surviving Nazi leaders, SS bodyguards, soldiers, Hitler's secretaries and cook crept away under cover of darkness – and into captivity, or history.

Organised resistance ceased on the morning of 2 May, although a die-hard group of Germans held out in the basement of the Reichstag for a few hours longer. Far above their heads, a 28-year old Ukrainian Jew working for the Tass news agency clambered on to the roof. Yevgheny Khaldei[89] was an enterprising war photographer armed with a Leica given to him by the legendary Robert Capa. Fired up by Joe Rosenthal's famous picture of US Marines raising the flag on Iwo Jima, he had made several red flags from table-cloths for just this moment. As German resistance sputtered out, Khaldei persuaded a Russian soldier called Alexei Kovalyov to perch precariously over the edge, his legs held by a soldier from Dagestan (wearing watches on both wrists – one was airbrushed out of the final picture by Soviet censors). Kovalyov unfurled the flag, Khaldei pressed the shutter and the final image of Hitler's war was created – the red banner floating in the wind above the ruins of Berlin.

NOTES

INTRODUCTION

1   The German army suffered 6.1 million casualties on the Russian Front between June 1941 and March 1945; twice the number of men that took part in the initial invasion and 80 per cent of German casualties over that period. Omer Bartov, *Hitler's Army*, Oxford University Press 1991.

2   Walter D. Dunn, Jr., *Hitler's Nemesis: The Red Army 1930–45*, Praegar 1994.

3   *The Trial of the Major German War Criminals*, 1946, Vol. 26, quoted in Klaus Fischer, *Nazi Germany*, London 1995.

CHAPTER ONE

4   'German Air Force Operations in support of the Army', General der Flieger a. D. Paul Deichman, *USAF Studies* 153, USAF Historical Division 1962.

CHAPTER TWO

5   From *The Russian Air Force in the Eyes of German Commanders*, Generalleutnant a. D. Walter Schwabedissen, USAF Historical Section, 1960.

6   Dimitri Volgonov, *Triumph and Tragedy*, London 1994.

7   Robert Conquest, *The Great Terror*.

8   Norman Stone, *The Eastern Front*, London 1975.

9   Harold Shukman (Ed.) *Stalin's Generals*, London 1993.

10 Russian acroynm for 'Chief Administration of Corrective Labour Camps'.

11 Bryan Fulgate and Lev Dvoretsky, *Thunder on the Dnepr*, Presidio Press, 1997.

CHAPTER THREE

12 Stavka Glavno Komandovaniya (High Command Headquarters) was created by the Central Committee on 23 June. To be chaired by Stalin, it consisted of the Marshals of the USSR, Chief of the General Staff, service chiefs from the navy and air arms etc. It was based in the Kremlin.

13 General der Flieger Paul Deichman, 'German Air Force operations in support of the Army', *USAF Studies* 153, USAF Historical Division, 1962.

14 The standard load was 430 tons of fuel for a Panzer division at full establishment. An additional 400–500 tons were carried by the Panzer and mechanised divisions in 1941, enabling them to make a fighting advance of 250–300 miles.

15 Operational report from Einsatzgruppe C, 2 November 1941.

16 See Omer Bartov, *The Eastern Front 1941–45: German troops and the barbarisation of warfare*, New York 1986 and *Hitler's Army*, New York 1991.

17 Robert H Jackson, Chief of Counsel for the United States in his opening statement at the first Nuremberg trial, 21 November 1945.

18 The definitive study of Soviet mobilisation is Walter S. Dunn, *Hitler's Nemesis: The Red Army, 1930–45*, Praegar 1994.

19 The strange disparity between German automotive manufacturing capability and military production is revealed by Richard Overy in *Why the Allies Won*, London 1995.

20 Martin van Creveld, *Supplying War: Logistics from Wallenstein to Patton*, Cambridge 1977.

CHAPTER FOUR

21 Quoted in John Erickson, *The Road to Stalingrad*, London 1975.

22 Modern estimates vary from 3.2 to 3.9 million. 16 generals were captured too with another 19 missing in action. See John Erickson's essay in *A Time to Kill*, London 1997.

23 Matthew Cooper, *The Phantom War*, London 1979.

24 Professor Richard Overy, *Why the Allies Won*, London 1995.

25 An underestimate: the Red Army fielded about six million men and women at the front from 1942–45. Fremde Heer Ost under the painstaking Colonel Gehlen consistently under-estimated Red Army strengths by a margin of about 500,000 although its assessment of the Soviet order of battle compares incredibly well with post-war documentation: the Germans were out by only seven divisions over the four years of war. See Walter S Dunn, *Hitler's Nemesis* p.43.

26 Total Luftwaffe strength in June 1942: 1,237 bombers, 369 dive-bombers, 278 Me-110 twin-engine fighters, 1,253 Me-109 fighters, 486 recce aircraft, 529 transports and 112 sea planes.

27 Not 'von Paulus' as many writers continue to call him. Like Walther Model (another favourite of Hitler's) he was a technocrat, not an aristocrat, which was more likely to endear him to the Führer who had little time for the blue-blooded officer corps.

CHAPTER FIVE

28 Erickson, The Road to Stalingrad, p.403.

29 Tank/assault gun strengths were: 14th Panzer Division, 41; 16th Panzer Division, 31; 24th Panzer Division, 55; 3rd Infantry Division, 32; 60th Infantry Division, 21.

30 The truth was even grimmer: Soviet tank production exceeded 2,000 tanks per month in 1942.

31 See Paul Carrell *Stalingrad and the defeat of the German 6th Army*, Schiffer Publishing, 1993, for an unreconstructed view of Hitler's responsibility.

He assigns further blame to Hitler, criticising the decision to withhold 29 divisions in the west including the three SS Panzer-grenadier Divisions, and 6th and 7th Panzer Divisions. He claims that just a quarter of this force could have liquidated the Russians in Stalingrad.

32 'Airlift operations', Generalmajor a.D. Fritz Morzik, *USAF historical studies* No.167, 1961.

33 Understandable for the men Milch inspected: they had just been transferred from North Africa!

34 Paulus' last active command had been that of an armoured reconnaissance unit in 1934. Paulus had never commanded a regiment, division or corps in action.

35 *When Titans Clash*, David M Glantz and Jonathan M House, University of Kansas Press, 1995, p.136–9.

36 In *Stalingrad – memories and reassessments* (London 1990) Joachim Wieder and Heinrich Graf von Einsiedel argue that only Manstein could have saved the 6th Army, by demanding permission to retreat from Stalingrad on 24 November and threatening to resign if Hitler refused. Would Hitler have accepted the loss of one of his greatest generals? Or did Manstein support Hitler's decision to hold the city so that he could be the saviour of the 6th Army?

37 Major-General von Mellenthin's famous account *Panzer Battles* (London 1955) concludes his account of the Stalingrad battle with 'the tactical conduct of the battle by the Russians was on a high level.'

38 Alexander Werth, *Russia at War 1941–45*, Barrie & Rockliff, 1964, p.506.

39 Paulus entitled his account 'Here I stand under orders'; the classic defence.

40 Marshal Chuikov, *The Beginning of the Road*, London 1963.

CHAPTER SIX

41 So memorably recounted in Guy Sajer's *Le Soldat Oublié*, Robert Laffont 1967, translated as *The Forgotten Soldier* and still in print both sides of the Atlantic (USA, Brassey's; UK, Orion).

42 These Bundesarchiv figures do not include SS casualties or losses after January 1945 when administration broke down. Another 500,000 losses were probably incurred before May. Of the nearly two million missing-in-action, at least half were dead.

43 *Why the Allies won*, Professor Richard Overy, p.188.

44 Manufacturing figures vary significantly (see introductory note regarding statistics) but even expressing it roughly like this reveals just how sluggish German aircraft production was compared to that of the Allies.

45 The Me-109 received successive upgrades to keep it in front-line service until 1945, and over 30,000 were built (more than almost any other aircraft of the war). However, its narrow undercarriage and unforgiving flight characteristics led to almost half of them being lost in training accidents.

46 In *RAF Bomber Command 1939–45: Reaping the Whirlwind*, Harper Collins 1996, Richard Overy demonstrates how the bombing of Germany not only checked Speer's attempt to expand production, but diverted enormous resources away from the fronts in Russia and Italy to the defence of the Reich itself.

47 General der Flieger Paul Deichman, 'German Air Force Operations in support of the Army' *USAF Studies* No.153, USAF Historical Division 1962.

48 General der Flieger Paul Deichman, 'German Air Force Operations in support of the Army' *USAF Studies* No.153, USAF Historical Division 1962.

49 *Panzertruppen* Vol II, Thomas L. Jentz, Schiffer Military History 1996, p.43.

50 *The Road to Berlin*, John Erickson, London 1983, p.82–4.

51 *Panzertruppen* Vol II, Thomas L Jentz, Schiffer Military History 1996. These are monthly inventories including all newly-built and not yet delivered vehicles, but they are much higher than the orders of battle the author quotes on p.176 (forces in the West, June 1944) and p.205 (forces in the East, May–June 1944).

52 Includes production totals for Panzer III and IV, Panther, Tiger, Tiger II tanks; Marder II and III and Nashorn self-propelled anti-tank guns; StuG III and IV, Hetzer, Elefant, Jagdpanzer IV, Jagdpanther and Jagdtiger assault guns; Wespe, Hummel, Brummbar and Sturmtiger self-propelled guns.

53 The best recent account is Richard Woodman's *Arctic Convoys*, John Murray 1994.

54 Although some sources quote over 6,000 (see footnote 3).

55 Nunn, *Hitler's Nemesis* p.158–61.

56 Although an SS battlegroup committed to Finland was expanded into the 6th SS Division during 1942 and the mounted SS regiments in Poland became 8th SS Division Florian Geyer. The 7th SS (Prinz Eugen) was an anti-partisan unit recruited in the Balkans where it spent most of the war.

57 *The Russian Revolution: A Peoples' Tragedy*, Orlando Figes, Jonathan Cape 1996.

58 Generalleutnant a. D. Klaus Uebe, 'Russian reactions to German airpower', *USAF Historical Studies* No.176.

CHAPTER SEVEN

59 Even then, there was not enough room. Some former Nazi concentration camps were put back into use by the Soviets to hold not just German captives but former Soviet soldiers and workers deported by the Germans for slave labour. The Soviet regime firmly believed that it was better to let 99 innocent men hang than let one guilty man go free.

60 John Erickson, *The Road to Berlin*, London 1983 p.48. They had lost 90 tanks in the previous two days, and the South-West Front had lost half its tanks to damage or breakdown before the German counter-attack was delivered.

61 Gerhard L Weinburg, *A World at Arms*, Cambridge 1994.

62 The Red Army had 27 artillery divisions by July 1943. It had about 100,000 mortars and anti-tank guns in service too.

63 Glantz and House, *When Titans Clash*.

64 Used by (among many others) Geoffrey Jukes, *Kursk*, Macdonald 1969.

65 Dimitri Volkogonov's *Stalin* supports Rokossovsky's revelations, quoting interviews with senior survivors of Kirponos' staff. Rokossovsky's memoirs were published after his death in 1968, but the degree to which they had been censored has only recently been exposed. See Richard Woff's essay in Harold Shukman (Ed.) *Stalin's Generals*.

66 John Erickson, *The Road to Berlin*, p.112.

67 'German Air Force Operations in support of the Army', General der Flieger a. D. Paul Deichman, USAF Historical Division, 1962.

68 F.W. Mellenthin, *Panzer Battles*, University of Oklahoma Press, 1956.

CHAPTER EIGHT

69 Partisans were also swept into the Red Army as areas were liberated, but about 20 per cent had to be rejected on medical grounds. Tuberculosis was commonly cited.

70 John Erickson gives the Soviet figure for German manpower (4.9 million) which has proved to be a massive over-estimate. On the other hand, the Germans underestimated Soviet manpower, believing they faced five million Soviet troops.

71 Thomas Jentz *Panzertruppen* Vol II cites German tank unit returns of 2,053 tanks (1,043 operational) in December 1943. This does not include assault guns. However, the divisional unit strengths he quotes on p.205 add up to a grand total of only 1,390 tanks and StuGs for May 1944. Since Panzeroffizier beim Chef Generalstab des Heeres Nr.561/44 GK, *Captured German Records*, Series T-78, Roll 620 shows German operational strength fluctuating between 400 and 600 tanks and about 700 assault guns on the Russian front from the end of September 1943 to early May 1944, it seems more likely that the total armoured strength of the Ostheer (including tanks, StuGs and other tank destroyers/assault guns) was no more than 1,500 at the beginning of 1944. Note also that despite prodigious production totals, Soviet frontline tank strength had fallen from 8,500 at the beginning of 1943 to 5,600 in December.

72 John Erickson states that the Germans had 54,000 guns and mortars, a figure that presumably includes 8.1cm and smaller weapons within divisions: Glantz and House *When Titans Clash* p.184 credits the Germans with 8,037 guns and mortars. Production figures indicate that the Soviets could well have enjoyed a 5:1 superiority in heavy artillery by early 1944. The Soviet attack on Army Group Centre in 1944 involved over 25,000 guns, mortars and rocket launchers.

73 The German total is from Generalleutnant Herman Plocher, 'The German Air Force in Russia', *USAF Historical Study* 154, 1966. John Erickson gives 8,818 aircraft for the Russians, but 'The Russian Air Force in the eyes of German commanders', Generalleutnant Walter Schwabedissen, *USAF Historical Studies* 1960, credits the Soviets with 13,000 aircraft in January 1944, rising to 20,000 by the end of the year despite monthly losses of 1,500 aircraft at the front and 1,200 in the rear.

74 Always a relative term in the Ukraine. Mevin lies at 273m above sea level. Heading west, it marks the start of the higher ground (always over 200m) of the western Ukraine that extends all the way to the foothills of the Carpathians.

75 A three-battalion brigade formed and led by Belgian Fascist leader Léon Dégrelle, the Wallonien brigade fought under Wehrmacht control until 1943 when it was transferred to the SS. Of the 2,000 men trapped at Cherkassy, 632 managed to escape to form the nucleus of 28th Panzer Grenadier Division Wallonien, which fought on until 1945.

76 Alexander Werth, *Russia at War*.

77 *The Trial of German Major War Criminals: Proceedings of the International Military Tribunal sitting at Nuremberg, Germany*, London 1946-51, Vol 21 p.72.

78 Omer Bartov, *Hitler's Army*, Oxford 1992, p.130. Space precludes a fuller examination of the Nuremberg trials, but the Western Allies' treatment of German war criminals was lopsided. Rocket engineers went free to work for the US government. Then again, some of the Soviet prosecutors had provided the required legal veneer to Stalin's purges. Vae Victis …

79 Gerhard Weinberg, *A World at Arms*, Cambridge 1994.

80 With the Royal Navy still dominating the Mediterranean, the German naval units reached the Black Sea from Hamburg; travelling up the River Elbe to Dresden where they were partially dismantled and driven along the highway to Ingolstadt, thence to Linz and down the length of the Danube.

CHAPTER NINE

81 Panzeroffizier beim Chef Generalstab des Heeres, Nr. 561/44 GK, *Captured German Records*, Series T-78, Roll 620. Much higher figures – over 4,000 – are sometimes quoted, but probably include new production and unserviceable vehicles, they may even be counting rebuilt vehicles twice. The Ostheer had at least another 700 tanks on its strength in May 1944 but they were not operational.

82 Alexander Werth, *Russia at War*, London 1964, p.768.

83 A one-time army colleague of the SS Chief-of-Staff Gottleb Berger, Dirlewanger enjoyed Himmler's patronage and was awarded some of Germany's highest medals for gallantry. He was killed in 1945 and his unit wiped out during the battle for Berlin.

84 Stephen Constant, *Foxy Ferdinand: Tsar of Bulgaria*, London 1979, p.329.

CHAPTER TEN

85 Quoted in John Toland, *The Last 100 Days*, London 1965, p.188.

86 John Toland, *The Last 100 Days*, London 1965. See also John Erickson, *The Road to Berlin*, p.508 and Alexander Werth, *Russia at War*, p.963–6 and 986.

87 James P. O'Donnell, *The Berlin Bunker*, London 1979, Chapter 7.

88 In *Hitler: a study in tyranny* and *Hitler and Stalin: parallel lives*, Alan Bullock demonstrates the extraordinary consistency of Hitler's beliefs from his writings and speeches of the 1920s to his 'final testament' dictated on 29 April.

89 His mother was shot by a Ukrainian mob while he was just 12 months old, the bullet passing through his side to kill her. His father was beaten to death in a subsequent pogrom. The Germans killed his sisters. It is pleasant to record that in his final years he received recognition in the west, and met the famous Associated Press photographer whose work had so inspired him. Khaldei died in October 1997.

INDEX

SELECT BIBLIOGRAPHY

Adelman, Jonathan and Gibson, Cristann (Ed.s) *Soviet Military Affairs: The Legacy of World War II*, Boston, 1989.

Addison, Paul and Calder, Angus (Ed.s) *Time to Kill*, London, 1997.

Andrew, Christopher and Gordievsky, Oleg *KGB: The Inside Story*, London, 1990.

Bartov, Omer *The Eastern Front 1941–45, German troops and the Barbarization of Warfare*, New York, 1986.

Bartov, Omer *Hitler's Army*, New York, 1991.

Bekker, Cajus *The Luftwaffe War Diaries*, London, 1967.

Bekker, Cajus *Hitler's Naval War*, London, 1976.

Berenbaum, Michael *Witness to the Holocaust*, New York, 1997.

Bishop, Christopher and Drury, Ian (Ed.s) *War Machine*, London, 1983–5.

Bishop, Christopher and Drury, Ian (Ed.s) *Combat Guns*, London, 1987.

Boldt, Gerhard *Hitler's Last Days*, London, 1973.

Brown, Eric *Wings of the Luftwaffe*, London, 1977.

Bruce, Robert *German Automatic Weapons of World War II*, London, 1996.

Bullock, Alan *Hitler and Stalin*, London, 1993.

Butler, Rupert *Gestapo*, London, 1992.

Carrell, Paul *Stalingrad and the defeat of the German 6th Army*, Atglen, PA, 1993.

Chuikov, Vasili *The Beginning of the Road*, London, 1963.

Cooper, Matthew *The Phantom War*, London, 1979.

Conquest, Robert *The Great Terror.*

Creveld, Martin van *Supplying War: Logistics from Wallenstein to Patton*, Cambridge, 1977.

Creveld, Martin van *Fighting Power: German and US Army battlefield performance 1939–45*, London, 1983.

Dunn, Walter *Hitler's Nemesis: The Red Army 1930–45*, Westport CT, 1994.

Deichman, Paul *German Air Force Operations in Support of the Army*, USAF Historical Division, 1962.

Elkins, Michael *Forged in Fury*, Loughton, 1981.

Einsiedel, Heinrich Graf von *The Onslaught: The German Drive on Stalingrad*, London, 1984.

English, John *On Infantry*, New York, 1981.

Erickson, John *The Road to Stalingrad*, London, 1975.

Erickson, John *The Road to Berlin*, London, 1983.

Fest, Joachim *The Face of the Third Reich*, London, 1970.

Figes, Orlando *The Russian Revolution: A Peoples' Tragedy*, London, 1996.

Fischer, Klaus *Nazi Germany*, London, 1995.

Fulgate, Brian and Dvoretsky, Lev *Thunder on the Dnepr*, Novato CA, 1997.

Gallagher, Hugh Gregory *By Trust Betrayed: Patients, Physicians and the Licence to Kill in the Third Reich*, Arlington, VA, 1995.

Glantz, David *Soviet Military Deception in the Second World War*, London, 1989.

Glantz, David and House, Jonathan *When Titans Clashed*, Kansas, 1995.

Griess, Thomas *Atlas of the Second World War: Europe and the Mediterranean*, West Point Military History series, New Jersey, 1985.

Guderian, Heinz *Panzer Leader*, London, 1952.

Gudmundsson, Bruce *On Artillery*, Westport CT, 1993.

Hooton, E.R. *Eagle in Flames*, London, 1997.

Jentz, Thomas *Panzertruppen*, Atglen, PA, 1996.

Jukes, Geoffrey *Kursk*, London, 1969.

Keegan, John *Waffen SS: The Asphalt Soldiers*, London, 1970.

Lang, Jochen von *Bormann: The Man who Manipulated Hitler*, London, 1979.

Lewin, Ronald *Ultra*, London, 1980.

Lord Russell of Liverpool *The Scourge of the Swastika*, London, 1954.

Liddell Hart, Basil *The Other Side of the Hill*, London, 1950.

Manstein, Erich von *Lost Victories*, London, 1959.

Mellenthin, F.W. von *Panzer Battles*, London, 1955.

Morzik, Fritz 'Airlift operations', *USAF Historical Studies* No.167, 1961.

O'Donnell, James *The Berlin Bunker*, London, 1979.

Overy, Richard *The Air War 1939–45*, London, 1980.

Overy, Richard *Why The Allies Won*, London, 1995.

Overy, Richard *RAF Bomber Command 1939–45*, London, 1996.

Padfield, Peter *Himmler*, London, 1990.

Pipes, Richard *The Russian Revolution 1899–1919*, London, 1990.

Plocher, Herman 'The German Air Force in Russia', *USAF Historical Study* No. 154, 1966.

Sajer, Guy *The Forgotten Soldier*, New York, 1971.

Schwabedissen, Walter 'The Russian Air Force in the eyes of German commanders', *USAF Historical Studies*, 1960.

Sereny, Gitta *Albert Speer: His Battle with Truth*, London, 1995.

Shukman, Harold (Ed.) *Stalin's Generals*, London, 1993.

Simkin, Richard *Tank Warfare*, London, 1979.

Snyder, Louis *Encyclopedia of the Third Reich*, London, 1976.

Stone, Norman *The Eastern Front*, London, 1975.

Toland, John *Hitler*, New York, 1976.

Toland, John *The Last 100 Days*, New York, 1965.

Tsouras, Peter (Ed.) *Fighting in Hell*, London, 1995.

Tsouras, Peter (Ed) *The Anvil of War*, London, 1994.

The Trial of German Major War Criminals: Proceedings of the International Military Tribunal Sitting at Nuremberg, Germany, London, 1946–51.

Uebe, Klaus 'Russian reactions to German airpower', *USAF Historical Studies* No.176.

US Government Printing Office, *Handbook on German Military Forces*, Washington, 1945, reprinted by Louisiana University Press, 1990.

Volgonov, Dimitri *Triumph and Tragedy*, London, 1994.

Weinburg, Gerhard *A World at Arms*, Cambridge, 1994.

Werth, Alexander *The Year of Stalingrad*, London, 1946.

Werth, Alexander *Russia at War*, London, 1964.

Whiting, Charles *Gehlen: Germany's Master Spy*, New York, 1972.

Wieder, Joachim and Graf von Einsiedel, Heinrich *Stalingrad – memories and reassessments*, London, 1990.

Woodman, Richard *Arctic Convoys*, London, 1994.

Zank, Horst *Stalingrad, Kessel und Gefangenschaft,* Herford, 1993.

Zaloga, Steven and Grandsen, James *The Eastern Front: Armor Camouflage and Markings 1941–45*, London, 1983.